Trade Secrets of Washington Journalists

How to Get the Facts About What's Going on in Washington

"Didn't You Used To Be In The State Department?"

Trade Secrets of Washington Journalists

How to Get the Facts About What's Going on in Washington

by Steve Weinberg
Foreword by **Walter Cronkite**

Cartoons by Auth, Herblock, MacNelly, Oliphant, Rechin, Sanders, Trudeau

ACROPOLIS BOOKS LTD.
Washington, D.C. 20009

ACROPOLIS BOOKS LTD.
Colortone Building, 2400 17th St.,
N.W., Washington, D.C. 20009

Printed in the United States of America by
COLORTONE PRESS Creative Graphics, Inc.
Washington, D.C. 20009

Library of Congress Cataloging in Publication Data

Weinberg, Steve
  Trade Secrets of Washington Journalists

  1. Journalists — reporting methods.
2. Journalists — Washington, D.C. I. Title
II. index III. bibliography

ISBN 0-87491-424-8   81-66854

Table of Contents

Why They Come to Washington • What They Write
About • Where They Write It • Off-limits • Skirting
Barriers to Information-Gathering

The Media Galleries • The People on Capitol Hill •
Personal Finances • Campaign Finances •
Congressional Pay and Privileges • Personal Staff as
Privilege • The Member of Congress as Legislator • The
Workings of Committees and Subcommittees • Following
the Dollar Through Congress • Tracking Legislation
Through the House and Senate • The Support Staffs of
Congress

Accredited Journalists, Non-Accredited Investigators
and the Press Office • Covering News from the White
House • The White House Staff • Documents Useful for
Investigating the White House

Acknowledgments

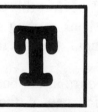his book covers so much that no journalist, no matter how capable an investigator, could have researched it without help. I had help from hundreds of people. Just some are mentioned here, but only for lack of space, not for lack of gratitude.

The book began as a project commissioned by the National Press Foundation. Vivian Vahlberg, a Foundation director and a Washington correspondent for the Oklahoma City newspapers, conceived the idea. From the first day, I received encouragement and constructive criticism from Vivian; from Frank Aukofer, Foundation president and Washington Bureau chief for the *Milwaukee Journal*; and from Arthur Wiese, Foundation vice president and Washington Bureau chief for the *Houston Post*. Don Larrabee, the Foundation's secretary and executive director, handled many of the logistics.

At Acropolis Books Ltd., Peter Spiers worked with me week in and week out, improving the copy. Alphons Hackl, president and publisher of Acropolis, buoyed me with his enthusiasm.

I owe a lot to the journalism graduate students from the University of Missouri who work with me in Washington, D.C. They have taught me as much as I have taught them. Two former students were of especial help on sections of the book—Paul Wilson, a political campaign consultant at Bailey Deardourff & Associates, and Lilah Lohr, a *Washington Star* reporter. Edmund Lambeth—former Washington correspondent and my predecessor as director of the School of Journalism's Washington Reporting Program, now teaching at Indiana University—was an inspiration and storehouse of knowledge.

The chapter on Congress was read in draft form by Carolyn Emigh, a former House and Senate staffer now in business as a consultant; the agencies chapter was read in draft form by Jeffrey Jacobs at the National Academy of Public Administration and John Scholzen at the U.S. Office of Personnel Management. Their comments were invaluable.

James Deakin, White House correspondent for the *St. Louis Post-Dispatch*, took time away from his book writing as a fellow at the Woodrow Wilson International Center for Scholars to critique my original outline.

The editorial cartoonists whose work appears in the book were gracious enough to grant permission for use of their labors.

My thanks also to the Washington correspondents for newspapers, periodicals and broadcast stations whose stories I used as examples of good reporting. Most of the journalists and non-journalists who sat still for interviews are not named here, but they know who they are. I would be negligent, however, unless I gave special recognition to David Broder and Lou Cannon of the *Washington Post*, Roy Gutman at Reuters, Robert Pierpoint at CBS News, Kent Cooper at the Federal Election Commission and Barrett McGurn at the U.S. Supreme Court.

Last but hardly least, I thank my wife Scherrie Goettsch and my daughter Sonia for their patience, support and love.

Foreword

hen I first came to Washington in 1948, the budget of the entire federal government was under $40 billion. On Capitol Hill, members of Congress had an average annual allowance of $2500 and only half a dozen staff people to assist them in passing the laws that govern our nation.

In those days, Washington was covered by a relatively small number of print and radio reporters. Television news was in its infancy; newspapers were all-powerful. Young reporters learned their craft as apprentices had always done—by watching and listening to the veterans.

It may be that the world was as complex to us then as it is to reporters now but there were fewer of us to dissect it. Now there are 4000 reporters, editors, photographers and technicians accredited to the press galleries, the White House, the State Department and the Pentagon. They cover a government with a budget of more than $700 billion annually. And on Capitol Hill, Congress spends more than a billion dollars a year just to keep itself operating. Most individual congressmen have at least twenty persons on their payroll.

Covering Washington, the way it is, has never been an easy task. A senator or congressman may specialize in an area or two with experts on his personal or committee staffs ready to supply essential information. A reporter rarely has such luxury. A typical Washington reporter can shift from covering agricultural price supports to foreign policy issues on a moment's notice.

Most of us learn the hard way. I suppose the new reporter in town back in 1948 managed to compete if he knew the way to the Senate and House press galleries, if he could find the waiting room for the press corps near the Oval Office at the White House or locate the news release rack at the National Press Club. There was no guide book for the beginner and no one felt the need for one because the federal government was an almost manageable beat.

But the challenge, then as now, is in obtaining the basic information quickly and accurately and in conveying it with a minimum of distortion. Only the beat has broadened.

However, in the Washington that the late Peter Lisagor fondly referred to as a pressure-cooker, there is seldom, if ever, the time for a reporter or editor to learn the beat in its entirety. The correspondent may figure out how to get from here to there in the expanding greater Washington area but he is taxed to digest the information needed to get the story done before moving on to yet another complex subject.

With the passage of years, the reporter develops that all-important sense of where to go to get information. He finds and cultivates his sources. These are his secrets—and they are the secrets of everyone in journalism.

This handbook for Washington journalists, commissioned by the National Press Foundation, may not reveal all the sources but I venture that most of those detailed by Steve Weinberg will be recognizable to the professional Washington reporter. They are among the most valuable tools of the trade.

Walter Cronkite

CROCK

by Bill Rechin & Don Wilder

Introduction

ore first-rate journalists congregate in Washington, D.C. than in any other city in the world. Yet the quality of reporting from Washington is often harshly criticized.

One reason is that the federal government is difficult to cover well. "Washington is the quintessential insiders' town," says Steve Rattner of the *New York Times* Washington Bureau. "There's a shorthand and you have to learn it. For a journalist, learning how the White House press office functions or where the Capitol stenographers hang out is no more difficult than navigating New York's subways—except that Washington's procedural corridors remain unmapped."

This book is my attempt to map those corridors. It is a reflection of my belief that many stories written by Washington correspondents are superficial (or never written at all) because reporters seldom have time to learn how things work in this city. They frequently are unaware that valuable information even exists.

A study of the Washington media by Stephen Hess (published in 1981 as *The Washington Reporters*) revealed that correspondents rarely use documents, other than news releases and newspaper clippings, as background for their stories. Instead, they rely heavily on interviews. Their stories focus on isolated events that occurred yesterday or today or will occur tomorrow—an announcement by the president, a congressional committee hearing or a court decision.

That kind of reporting has its place. But so much more can be discovered if a correspondent knows the way Washington works. In 1980, Ted Gup and Jonathan Neumann of the *Washington Post* examined consulting contracts awarded by government agencies. They could have spent a few days interviewing and then written a story. Instead, they scrutinized all 13,848 contract awards for 1979, totaling $9.3 billion. In doing so, they discovered that more than two-thirds of the contracts had been awarded without competition. Armed with an overview and specific cases of apparent abuse, Gup and Neumann then began interviewing. They talked to obvious sources, but they also talked to prostitutes hired by private consultants to influence the conduct of officials. When confronted by the evidence Gup and Neumann had compiled, government officials admitted wrongdoing to the reporters. The series that resulted led to congressional hearings, legislation and disciplinary action against federal bureaucrats.

Another reporter not easily satisfied is Gaylord Shaw of the *Los Angeles Times* Washington Bureau. Shaw was writing follow-up stories on the 1976 collapse of the Teton Dam: "I was struck," he said," by the fact that federal officials insisted that Teton was the best dam they had ever built. If that was the case, I wondered, then what about the Bureau of Reclamation's other 300 big dams?"

Shaw broke away from other assignments to investigate. "Before long," he wrote in the *Investigative Reporters and Editors Journal*, "I found in government files a raft of engineering documents showing that, for at least a dozen years, officials had known that a score of big Bureau of Reclamation dams had serious safety problems." The White House formed a multi-agency group to alter dam safety procedures, and Congress approved money for an investigation.

A Washington correspondent need not work at a giant newspaper for months on one story to do a thorough job. In 1980, as a freelancer for a monthly magazine, I wrote a profile of a congressman. Even though I held a regular job, and had to do the story in stolen moments, I did not rely on quick interviews with obvious sources.

The congressman chaired a committee, so a major part of my assignment was to determine his relationship to the special interests that fell within the committee's jurisdiction. One of the first places I visited was the Library of Congress. There, on a computer terminal, I ordered a free printout of every bill the congressman had introduced since becoming committee chairman. From the printout I was able to tabulate how many bills were intended to aid the special interests.

Before conducting any interviews, I obtained the congressman's annual financial disclosure, his campaign finance reports, every news release issued by the committee since he had become chairman, the committee's budgets and annual reports, vote ratings of the congressman from a dozen private groups and more.

When, finally, it was time to conduct interviews, I talked to obvious and not-so-obvious sources: members and former members of the committee, Democratic and Republican committee staffers, lobbyists from a half-a-dozen groups that regularly requested legislation from the committee, adminstration officials who worked closely with the committee, constituents of the congressman who lived in a distant state, journalists who covered him regularly and others. The result was a rich, controversial story that was avidly read and brought calls to me as well as letters to the magazine.

At the time I began this book for the National Press Foundation, I was writing it primarily for newcomers to Washington reporting who were interested in learning about useful, not-so-obvious sources of information—the kinds used by Gup, Neumann, Shaw and myself. I imagined how such a book would have helped me when I arrived in Washington as a reporter, with no one to guide me. Soon the project began to grow into something more than a manual for newcomers. As I delved deeper into my research, I realized how many discoveries I was making. Other longtime Washington correspondents did, too. Reading rough drafts of my manuscript, they exclaimed how surprised they were to find the information lodes I had included, sources which previously had been unknown even to them. (The correspondents who read the rough drafts were male and female. Despite the use of the masculine gender throughout the book when referring to investigators, I am fully aware of how many top reporters in Washington are women. The masculine gender is used for readability only.)

The intended audience for the book expanded still more after numerous conversations with non-journalists. Gradually, I became aware that even those people who had never set foot inside a newsroom needed occasionally to probe behind the facade of the federal government. From the pages that follow, university students, scholars, lobbyists, public affairs practitioners, citizen group volunteers and others will be able to extract useful tips on how to dig out information. General readers, including those who consider themselves media watchers, will become more knowledgeable about how journalists in Washington operate—how they cover what they cover and why, sometimes, they fail to find certain stories.

Still, the question may legitimately be asked: Why is this book really needed? After all, Washington correspondents are the best that journalism has to offer. They are often veterans who have proved themselves back home by covering the state legislature or other important beats. They frequently have waited years, sometimes decades, for an opening in a Washington bureau, and once achieving their goal, have gained in experience, rarely leaving Washington voluntarily.

Yet much about Washington reporting remains to be criticized. One magazine for journalists, The Quill, published a report in 1978 entitled "Washington Neglected: What the Capital's 2500-Strong Press Corps Fails to Report." The authors studied stories and interviewed several dozen reporters and officals before concluding that coverage of the Cabinet departments and independent agencies was "inadequate or non-existent." Furthermore, the article said that even the White House, Congress and Pentagon were poorly covered. As for scandal, top investigative reporters overlooked numerous clues that could have led them to the illegal influence-peddling of Tongsun Park, the South Korean lobbyist.

Critics such as Tom Wicker of the New York Times have said repeatedly that too many stories with Washington datelines come from obvious, official sources. But when Wicker was Washington Bureau chief for the Times, with thirty reporters to deploy, he had difficulty doing things differently. "It is very hard to know what to do with those thirty reporters," he says. "When they are sent out to cover institutions and spokesmen, they inevitably miss a lot of other things that are happening. Also, the newspaper tends to take on a very heavy institutional flavor. And, as we found out in the 1960s, the institutions themselves often do not know what is happening."

Washington Post White House correspondent Lou Cannon, author of Reporting: An Inside View, notes that reliance on official governmental sources has not diminished despite the practice of government lying during Vietnam and Watergate. Even when Washington correspondents discover a previously unreported niche they may not paint a true picture. Cannon reports that almost every journalist who has gone to work for the federal government agrees it looks different from the inside.

This book is intended to help investigators understand the ins and outs of Washington reporting. The book is purposefully selective—everything included was included with this in mind: Will it help an investigator find useful information?

Decisions about what to include were based on my practical experience as a Washington correspondent; on ideas gathered from thousands of books, articles and documents; and on interviews with journalists, government officials and non-governmental experts.

A warning is appropriate here: What follows is not a directory of names and telephone numbers. There are already excellent directories yet each suffers from the same shortcoming—it is outdated within months. Of course, some of this book, too, will inevitably become outdated. Laws are amended. Disclosure forms are eliminated or modified. But what is written here is intended to be as timeless as possible. It is designed to describe processes and offer sources of information that, if known and understood, should help anybody do a better job of observing in Washington, D.C.

Chapter I and the related appendices provide an overview of the Washington news corps. The material is intended to help reporters (especially newcomers) in all media understand where they fit in. It is also meant to help news sources understand the media. Researchers, too, should find the cataloging of uncommon publications and broadcast services useful. The chapter examines how journalists work, what they write, and why they come to Washington. It explains aids to information-gathering and warns of barriers that exist for journalists and non-journalists alike.

Beginning with Chapter II, the book looks at Washington reporting, institution by institution. Many sections explore what is virgin terrain to most investigators—for example, the U.S. Tax Court, or executive branch advisory commissions. For reporters, editors and others who choose to skip around, the detailed table of contents will be a help. Specialists interested in looking at subjects outside their realm of experience will also find it beneficial.

The Washington Correspondents

t first glance, the number of Washington correspondents seems enormous. In what other American city do thousands of journalists report on government and public policy? Official congressional galleries alone accredited 3300 people to cover the House and Senate in 1981, and hundreds of unaccredited journalists roamed Capitol Hill in search of news, too.

But the vast majority of American newspapers, magazines and broadcast stations do not have their own employees in Washington, D.C. Furthermore, many accredited journalists are not reporters at all; they are editors, broadcast executives and camera crew technicians who never write a word about the federal government. Even accredited reporters cover the agencies, the courts and other institutions only sporadically.

Those journalists who do try to convey what the government is doing are fighting a losing battle. "The economics of the print medium guarantee that the government cannot be terribly well covered," says syndicated columnist George Will. "Relatively few newspapers can be represented in Washington bureaus, and most of those bureaus are very small. Consider the impact of a five-person, ten-person or even fifteen-person bureau on an enormous, complicated government such as this." As for television bureaus, Will says "the very nature of its technology makes television a slave to the camera, which is an inherently superficial news-gathering instrument."

Readers who want to interpret this as a condemnation of American journalism can do so. But the point to be emphasized is that the federal government is not covered by most media outlets (see Appendix I).

Why They Come to Washington

Among many journalists, working in Washington is the pinnacle, media Mecca. Students who have dreamed of reporting on a big daily newspaper come to Washington for an academic semester and never leave. They accept jobs on obscure trade publications, giving up their dreams of daily newspaper journalism, to remain near the seat of power. Reporters on small dailies in the Midwest quit and move to Washington with no prospects, knowing they will have to knock on doors for weeks, maybe months, before receiving a regular paycheck again. Why? Washington is "where the action is."

Sometimes the *Washington Post* is the goal. The Bob Woodward story has been told before. After failing to talk his way onto the *Post*, Woodward settled for a job on a suburban weekly. Despite his lack of newspaper experience, he pestered *Post* editors until they hired him for the unglamorous police beat. The story is atypical only in that Woodward did get hired, and in that he later helped expose the Watergate scandal in Richard Nixon's White House. A more recent Woodward-type saga at the *Post* is that of Ted Gup, an investigative reporter gaining recognition for his periodic blockbusting series. Gup decided at least seven years before he was hired by the *Post* that he would work there someday. Meeting with editors there, he plotted a course. Newspaper jobs in Ohio and Virginia, obtaining a law degree—Gup did it all with an eye on a *Post* job.

Tom Wicker, now of the *New York Times*, first came to Washington as a reporter for a daily in North Carolina. In his book *On Press*, Wicker describes how, at the start, he was intimidated by the famous politicians and journalists in Washington. But by the time Wicker was supposed to return to North Carolina—less than a year later—he rejected the idea of going back. Wicker's brief experience on the periphery of power had turned his head. Several years later, he was in Washington, working in the *New York Times* bureau, where a North Carolina colleague was news editor.

Wicker's reaction is common. Other journalists have enjoyed the switch to higher status. Journalists know Walter Lippmann had a role in drafting President Woodrow Wilson's Fourteen Points. Ben Bradlee had a close relationship with President John Kennedy, even though it may be that Kennedy sometimes used Bradlee. George Will hosted a party for President-elect Ronald Reagan. Arthur Krock, counselor to chiefs of state during many years in Washington with the *New York Times*, referred to his title "the Washington correspondent" as "elegant," and remarked on the professional and social prestige of the position.

Even journalists who never become counselors to presidents achieve social and professional prestige. Washington correspondents for ABC, CBS and NBC are known by millions across the United States. Covering political campaigns, they are sometimes besieged by more autograph-seekers than are the candidates. Being in the Washington bureau means air time, because the nightly network news is weighted toward events in the capital. Robert Pierpoint of CBS News has never attained the star status of Dan Rather or Roger Mudd, but after twenty-three years covering the White House, Pierpoint was certainly a celebrity of sorts. Even in 1980, when he switched to the State Department beat, his reporting continued to get play before huge audiences.

Though some journalists leave Washington, for many it becomes a lifetime assignment. There is no thought of rotating through and returning home—Washington is home. According to researcher Stephen Hess in his book *The Washington Reporters*, job satisfaction is high; stories tend to get good play, and usually are self-initiated; the hours are not terribly long; and routine office work is minimal.

The well-respected Washington bureau of the *Des Moines Register* is a microcosm of those who have left Washington and those who have stayed.

The bureau chief, James Risser, arrived in 1969, stayed, and won two Pulitzer Prizes for national reporting. Before Risser, bureau chiefs Clark Mollenhoff and Richard Wilson (also winners of Pulitzers for national reporting) stayed for decades.

On the other hand, James O'Shea, after just a few years, left the Washington bureau of the *Register* in the late 1970s to join the *Chicago Tribune*. He left even though his reporting of Congress and the executive branch agencies was regarded as top-notch.

Margaret Engel came to the *Register* Washington Bureau shortly after the departure of O'Shea. She was part of what appears to be a trend—younger reporters getting a Washington assignment without putting in a decade or more in the city room. Engel began on a medium-sized Ohio daily, and shifted to the *Register* in 1976. Just a couple of years later, she won a Nieman fellowship, probably the most prestigious in journalism. So she took a year off and joined the other Nieman fellows at Harvard University. When the year ended, Engel returned to Des Moines briefly, but wanted new challenges. Still several years shy of age thirty, she applied for and got a job in the Washington bureau. In early 1981, after about a year as a Washington correspondent, Engel said she had learned a great deal. But she did not have stars in her eyes. Nor did she see Washington as a lifelong assignment. Engel had discovered a few special satisfactions about Washington correspondence, such as "seeing policy made at the start," but overall did not perceive it as glamorous.

"I never had any awe or mystique about Washington," she said. "I had a negative image of Washington reporters—they seemed too dependent on handouts. I think there's still a mystique about Washington reporting 'out there,' but. . .that's unfortunate."

From the start, everyone is conditioned to route reporters to the press office, "so you have to work doubly hard to get to the people who really have the information," she said.

Though nearly half of the Washington correspondents surveyed by Hess said that news organizations should rotate reporters between Washington and the home office, few news organizations do that, and the rest are unlikely to change their policy.

What They Write About

A sizable number of Washington correspondents—especially the network news reporters—concentrate on national stories. They haunt the White House press room, informing the nation what the president said, who the president saw and where the president plans to vacation later in the month. They wait in the lobby of the State Department, hoping to question the secretary of state as he emerges from a meeting with a foreign minister visiting the United States. They attend news briefings at the Pentagon and ask about the military strength of America compared to that of the Soviet Union. They report on the latest scandal involving a multinational corporation released by the Securities and Exchange Commission. They bang out a story on a U.S. Supreme Court ruling that affects minority group hiring quotas. They watch Senate debate on an arms limitation treaty, or listen to the House of Representatives discuss a bill to raise Social Security taxes.

Such national stories are always easy to find and write, though doing them well is what separates the top national journalists from the run-of-the-mill correspondents. Hundreds of reporters, however, are in Washington to write stories for an audience with other than national interests. Those interests may be topical (university administrators who want details on congressional funding of student loan programs) or they may be geographical (how new Department of Agriculture regulations on price supports affect the Iowa corn grower).

The resourceful reporter who must specialize by topic or geography discovers sources—often by accident—which lead to exclusive stories of interest to his audience. In the rarely covered U.S. Tax Court, where cases are filed by state, James O'Shea, then a *Des Moines Register* Washington correspondent, made an interesting discovery in the Iowa file—the Internal Revenue Service had alleged that a stockholder-owned bank holding company there had purchased the house of its top officer for more then twice its market value. Further digging revealed that the house was later sold to a holding company director for half of what the company had originally paid.

"I tried to go through Tax Court files at least once a month," O'Shea said. "Usually I would find a story worth writing, and some of them were pretty good. I knew nothing about the bank-holding company story in advance. I saw a name I recognized and a dollar amount, so I decided to look at the whole file."

Many news releases from government agencies contain information broken down according to geographic location. A correspondent from a medium-sized paper might learn of a multi-million dollar Pentagon award to a local defense contractor by reading a release issued regularly by the Defense Department. If the Federal Communications Commission is thinking of revoking the license of a broadcast station, a Washington correspondent serving that distant city might learn about it by reading the station's file at the FCC, by having FCC news releases delivered to him daily or by reading the *Federal Register*. Data on population and housing from the Census Bureau often include revealing numbers for a Washington correspondent; little-noticed census reports for certain geographical areas are issued more often than the well-known ten-year national population counts. Budget proposals issued every January by the president can suggest stories for correspondents who specialize in geographical or in topical stories. The *Washington Post* has written stories on the effect the proposed budget would have on a particular congressional district, and on the fact that more than one-quarter of the budget would aid senior citizens.

Suggestions for source material could run dozens of pages. Another potential source is the local member of the House of Representatives. Still another is the Supreme Court and the various special courts in Washington, D.C: lawsuits can have a local as well as a national impact.

For those wishing to read model Washington stories, the winner's list of the National Press Club competition is available. Prizes are given to stories limited by geography and topic. In 1980, awards went to Eric Pianin and Finlay Lewis of the *Minneapolis Tribune* for a series on lobbying of organizations important to the Minnesota economy; to John Herbers of the *New York Times* for stories about the impact that government actions have on local areas (how Mobile, Alabama, adjusted to the loss of a military base); and to Joseph Volz of the *New York Daily News* for various stories relating to criminal justice and the law.

Where They Write It

Anybody can call himself a Washington correspondent. But reporters with official accreditation will have an easier time gathering information. The most important credentials are those from a congressional gallery, the White House, State Department and Defense Department. Credentials, and the working space that goes with them, are among the many privileges that journalists receive in Washington, D.C. Non-journalists who lack these privileges sometimes find it more difficult to obtain documents and interview sources. (Information about obtaining credentials as well as more about the advantages that go with them will be found throughout this book.)

Off-limits

Some places in Washington, D.C. are forbidden both to accredited journalists and the general public. Parts of almost every government building have restricted access. In the

Capitol, the House and Senate floors and cloakrooms are restricted areas. Otherwise, legitimate journalists can go almost anywhere, as long as they are not carrying a camera.

At the White House, almost every part of that building is off-limits. Accredited journalists or those who have been cleared on a one-time basis are permitted to go directly to the press area. A reporter wanting to go elsewhere in the White House complex must have an escort from the press office or an appointment with a source.

At the Supreme Court, much of the building is closed to outsiders, including reporters. On the first floor, closed areas are the justice's chambers and the access corridors to them; on the second and third floors, everything is closed to the public, including the law library, though an investigator with a specific interest might gain entry.

Generally, Cabinet department and independent agency buildings are open. But the Defense Department in the Pentagon is an exception. In many hallways, there are guards who halt members of the media and the public. Access beyond the guard is allowed only to Pentagon employees with the proper ID card.

The special obstacles that broadcasters face in getting film and sound are often insurmountable. The presence of these obstacles helps explain why the public does not see or hear certain things on television or radio news from Washington. For *TV Guide*, Ron Nessen, a former network news reporter and presidential press secretary, wrote that part of the problem is internal—television journalists fail to think of behind-the-scenes bargaining as grist for their newscasts.

But, Nessen added, "the major hindrance to covering a wider range of Washington stories is as simple as it is basic: Large areas of the Capitol, the White House and other public buildings are off-limits to TV cameras, or require cumbersome clearance procedures."

At the White House, the daily briefing conducted by the president's press secretary is open to broadcast reporters, but in most circumstances, only to those without their cameras. Cameras are restricted to the press room and to the north lawn between the press room and the northwest gate facing Pennsylvania Avenue.

In the Capitol buildings, too, there are restrictive policies on filming. Journalists may not film or record inside the House or Senate chambers, except with permission on special occasions. Those occasions include sessions when the House and Senate are joined for presidential addresses, and speeches by foreign dignitaries, astronauts and similar personages. House floor proceedings are now covered gavel-to-gavel, but the cameras are controlled by House employees. Some cable television systems show the entire proceedings, though in early 1981 broadcast networks and individual stations were using only infrequent excerpts. In early 1981, there was no televising of Senate floor proceedings although Majority Leader Howard Baker was hoping to change that.

Cameras are sometimes allowed inside committee and subcommittee hearings. Filming and recording of hearings usually requires permission, but permission is often routinely granted. The decision is made by the committee chairman. If there is an objection to allowing cameras in, a majority of the committee can override the objection. The House has a blanket rule on broadcast coverage of committees; its provisions are incorporated into each committee's own rules.

Generalizations concerning broadcaster access to executive branch departments and agencies are difficult to make. At the Defense Department in early 1981, camera crews were allowed to film in non-classified areas, but usually had to coordinate the filming with audiovisual specialists in the Pentagon media office. The Securities and Exchange Commission required advance permission from its secretary for photography, videotaping or tape recording. The Federal Energy Regulatory Commission allowed sound recordings to be made at its meetings, but still and movie cameras were allowed only without lighting aids.

Skirting Barriers to Information-Gathering

The Government in the Sunshine Act is one tool both journalists and non-journalists use to gain access to information that government officials would like to see withheld. "The Sunshine Act has facilitated our coverage of the agencies," says Richard Roth, a CBS Washington correspondent. "Most allow some broadcast coverage; if we need pictures of a body deliberating to go with a story, we can usually get them." But the act is not a magic passkey to all meetings—it does not cover Congress, the thirteen Cabinet departments or the White House. It does apply to about fifty agencies headed by more than one member, such as the Securities and Exchange Commission and the Federal Election Commission.

Many meetings are still closed, just as they were before the 1976 law. That is because the law contains ten exemptions to openness (see Appendix II). Numerous agencies use the exemptions as loopholes. During 1980, for example, the Securities and Exchange Commission was holding closed meetings nearly every Tuesday. Thursday meetings generally were open, Wednesday meetings open or closed depending on the agenda. Recent federal court decisions have held that agencies (including the Federal Communications Commission and the Council on Environmental Quality) were interpreting exemptions to the sunshine law too broadly. Monitoring by Common Cause turned up some agencies that close almost as many meetings as they open, including the National Labor Relations Board, Commodity Futures Trading Commission and Export-Import Bank. Nonetheless, the law has done more good than harm. Agencies are required, whenever it is possible, to make public announcements, even of closed meetings, at least a week in advance. Meeting notices are published in the *Federal Register*, and detailed agendas often are available through the mail to persons who request them.

The Freedom of Information Act (see Appendix III) is supposed to open government files, just as the sunshine law is supposed to open meetings. The law was approved in 1966 and amended signficantly in 1974. Journalists have filed thousands of requests under the law for withheld information, although businesses trying to obtain information about their competitors and other non-journalistic entities have used the law more than reporters. Like the Government in the Sunshine Act, the Freedom of Information Act does not apply to all branches of government. Congress is not covered under either law, nor is the judiciary. But the Freedom of Information Act does have broader application within the executive branch than does the Government in the Sunshine Act. Cabinet departments are covered; so is the Executive Office of the President.

Unfortunately for investigators the Freedom of Information Act is riddled with loopholes. Nine categories of information are exempted from disclosure. One of those exemptions is a loophole on top of a loophole which says that if information is specifically exempted from disclosure by a law other than the Freedom of Information Act, the Freedom of Information Act is superseded. As of 1981, there appeared to be at least 150 exemptions from the Freedom of Information Act written into other legislation. Nobody—not even the congressional subcommittees with jurisdiction over the law—knows for sure how many.

But investigators should not be discouraged by the problems resulting from the nine exemptions, from occasionally exorbitant agency search and photocopying fees or from agency dallying that can render information outdated for news purposes. Why not be discouraged? Because requests for information under the law can pay off handsomely. Sometimes the Freedom of Information Act officers in the executive branch (almost every department and agency has such an officer) help investigators obtain the information without a fight. There are appeals processes within each department and agency, and those appeals often bear fruit. Even if an appeal fails, there is recourse to the federal courts. A successful plaintiff might be awarded legal fees, as was Steve Aug of the *Washington Star* after obtaining information withheld by the National Railroad Passenger Corporation.

One testimonial to the Freedom of Information Act came from William Shawcross, author of the book *Sideshow*, which describes the bombing of Cambodia during the administration of Richard Nixon. Shawcross made numerous successful requests for confidential materials. The Department of Defense, State Department, Central Intelligence Agency, National Security Council and Agency for International Development gave him thousands of pages of documents whose classification ranged from confidential to top-secret, sensitive, eyes of addressee only, no foreigners. Carl Stern of NBC News used the law to obtain information for a story on secret FBI operations. Stern said he continues to use the law to obtain information even if he is unsure whether a story will result. "If I'm denied something wrongly, I'll pursue it as a matter of principle," Stern said. "Maybe the next time I need something in a hurry from the agency, I'll get it."

Using the Freedom of Information Act, Jack Taylor of the *Daily Oklahoman and Times* obtained documents enabling him to detail the Army's secret probe of the My Lai killings in Vietnam.

Taylor, a self-proclaimed FOI Act "junkie," estimated that during the 1970s he filed approximately 2500 requests at about fifty federal agencies. "Probably half my requests have led to the release of some or all of the documents I sought," Taylor said in the *Investigative Reporters and Editors Journal*. When information was concealed, Taylor found ways to get at it. "Army or other military censors in Washington would release documents sanitized simply by blacking out words or sentences with Crayolas. More frequently Bureau of Indian Affairs employees used the same method. Of course, a sharp knife scrapes away all their efforts," he said.

The Privacy Act of 1974 can also help an investigator gain information, but usually only about himself. Some agencies have used the Privacy Act (see Appendix IV) to deny requests for files containing names of individuals asked for under the Freedom of Information Act. To make sure he is not being denied information he is entitled to have, an investigator should acquaint himself with both laws before trying to use them. One of the clearest guides is published by the House Committee on Government Operations. *A Citizen's Guide on How to Use the Freedom of Information Act and the Privacy Act in Requesting Government Documents* is available for purchase through the Government Printing Office.

Because government agencies can hide behind top-secret stamps in evading requests for information under the Privacy Act or the Freedom of Information Act, it is important for investigators to know exactly what information is classified, by whom and how long it remains classified before entering the public domain. The problem is a thorny one. How can anyone know about a document that has been classified and not yet declassified? There is no systematic published record of such documents. From time to time reporters are handed classified documents by "leakers." The trouble is that such leaks are irregular and almost always occur because of an ulterior motive. In *On Press*, Tom Wicker of the *New York Times* reports that President Lyndon Johnson ordered aides to leak information to a reporter who was temporarily filling in for the White House regular. The reason? Johnson disliked the regular and wanted to make him look bad. Steve Rattner, a Washington correspondent for the *Times*, says sometimes an exclusive story results from deft reporting, but more often it starts with a leak that either "reflects the subject's desire to get the story out or an opponent's desire to attract attention to some offensive action."

President Jimmy Carter's 1978 Executive Order 12065 was an attempt to reform the classification system. It was designed to halt wrongful classification, what one U.S. senator was talking about when he said, "In practice classified information is material which some individual in government decides he does not want made public. He could make that decision to hide incompetence. Many have. He could be trying to conceal waste. Many have. He could even be attempting to camouflage corrupt behavior and improper influence. Many have. He could simply be covering up facts which might embarrass him or his bosses." The executive order limits classification to national security information. Such information can be stamped, if warranted, with one of only three designations: top-secret, secret or confidential.

Only certain people can wield the top-secret stamp: The president is one. Others are officials in the White House complex publicly designated by the president. Specified department and agency heads also have the privilege. Subordinates to these top officials can classify information top-secret under certain circumstances. There are longer lists of authorized classifiers for the secret and confidential categories. Although only national security information is eligible for classification, some of the national security definitions are broad. For instance, "scientific, technological or economic matters" relating to national security can be classified.

Classified documents must be declassified after six years. Many, however, remain secret for twenty years or more because of extensions granted by the head of the agency. An Information Security Oversight Office within the General Services Administration was created by executive order; it is supposed to monitor agencies that classify material. Each of these agencies has appointed someone who, with the help of classification instruction manuals, actively oversees implementation of the executive order.

Although a great deal of non-sensitive information is classified unnecessarily, there are regular calls for even tighter secrecy measures. Richard Halloran of the *New York Times* Washington Bureau reported in 1981 that a House subcommittee looking into the controversial release of information about the Stealth bomber concluded the Pentagon could be doing more to prevent security leaks.

Even when documents are classified and declassified according to the rules, investigators face the problem of knowing when previously classified material enters the public realm. There are ways to do that but none is easy. At the National Archives and Records Service, reference archivists will help investigators find declassified documents by subject matter. Millions of pages of documents each year are transferred by agencies to the Archives. Almost every document more than twenty years old is systematically reviewed.

In its quarterly journal *Prologue*, the National Archives reports on selected sets of records under review. For example, a recent issue of *Prologue* noted that "review of the 1945-49 central files of the State Department continued." Also under review was "the microfilmed World War II confidential and secret files of the Operations Division, War Department General Staff." The Central Intelligence Agency publishes a list of its unclassified publications available to the public.

By the time the documents enter the public domain, they are usually "history." But some still make good stories. In 1978, the *Los Angeles Times* ran a story about how, during the Korean War, a Cabinet-level group urged President Truman to begin a worldwide offensive against communism, including bombing the Chinese mainland. The story's source was a recently declassified report, stamped top-secret at the time it was filed in 1951. The document had been turned over to the National Archives along with other National Security Council papers from the 1940s, 1950s and 1960s.

There is at least one private company (Carrollton Press Inc. in Arlington, Virginia) that publishes collections of declassified documents. At the end of 1980, the company's Declassified Documents Reference System included over 18,000 items. The documents are chosen from those declassified under the mandatory review procedures of Executive Order 12065 or under the Freedom of Information Act. The copies are acquired from the originating agency (such as the State Department), the National Archives, or from one of the Presidential Libraries. The Library of Congress and several other Washington-area libraries carry the Carrollton collection. A full-service annual subscription cost $685 at the beginning of 1981.

The executive order governing classified materials does not cover Congress. As already noted, Congress has exempted itself from other tools of access—the Freedom of Information Act, Privacy Act and Government in the Sunshine Act. This should be a clue that Congress is a world unto itself. The next chapter examines Congress, suggesting how an investigator can discover information in that unique institution.

Congress

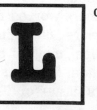

Lots of reporters cover Congress. But the way many of them do it provokes criticism. Easy stories on committee hearings, bill introductions and floor debate are the staples of coverage. But where, as a critic in the *Washingtonian* magazine asked, are the stories about the quiet death of important bills in subcommittee, or about subcommittee chairmen who use their authority to hand out favors and control the bureaucracy?

Congressional correspondents recognize the significance of these in-depth pieces, but say that keeping up with hearings and press releases leaves little time for digging. Yet, the *Washingtonian* article noted, when *Hustler* magazine publisher Larry Flynt testified at a hearing on pornography, the room was filled with reporters who wrote stories similar to those their editors received on the wires.

When covered sensibly, however, Congress can inspire good stories. "Everything starts in Congress," says James

Deakin, veteran Washington correspondent of the *St. Louis Post-Dispatch*. "Almost every issue germinates there. Besides, it's a microcosm of Washington. There's a hearing and a report on anything. The pressure groups that will be affected are all there in the hearing room." An investigator covering Congress will have an advantage if he has access to the media galleries.

The Media Galleries

The largest of the four galleries in Congress is for daily print journalists. In early 1981, the gallery had about 1350 accredited correspondents from about 675 media organizations. Most of the correspondents report for daily newspapers of general circulation. There are working areas on the House and Senate sides of the Capitol; accreditation to one is valid for both. (The same is true for the periodical and radio-television galleries, to be discussed below. The still photographers gallery has working space on the Senate side only.)

The daily press gallery is governed by five journalists, called the Standing Committee of Correspondents. They are elected for two-year terms. In 1981, the members worked for the *Houston Chronicle, New York Times, Baltimore Sun*, United Press International and *Washington Post*. Campaigning for the seats is sometimes heated, as chronicled in a first-person account by reporter Mick Rood in a 1979 issue of *The Washington Monthly*.

Like the other Congressional galleries, the press gallery is funded by Congress with taxpayer money—one of the perquisites for correspondents rarely mentioned in stories about perquisites of government officials. The salaries of the seven employees in the Senate gallery and five in the House gallery come from congressional appropriations. These twelve employees answer telephones for the journalists, keep track of debate on the House and Senate floors, post news releases from congressmen and issue briefs from Congress' political party groups, set up gallery news conferences for members of Congress who were key figures in a just-debated bill, manage media arrangements at crowded committee hearings, handle space for reporters at the Democratic and Republican national conventions and generally make reporting simpler for gallery members.

Few reporters spend their entire day in the gallery, but if they are covering House or Senate floor debate, they must enter the galleries that overlook the chambers through doors from the press gallery interior. During breaks in the debate, correspondents can re-enter the gallery and accomplish other tasks. When on Capitol Hill, some accredited reporters avoid the congestion of the main galleries by working from satellite galleries in the Rayburn and Longworth House Office Buildings and in the Russell Office Building on the Senate side.

Not just anyone can be accredited to work in these surroundings, however. Rules for eligibility are published in the *Congressional Directory*—a key prerequisite for gaining access to the press galleries is that an applicant's "principal income" must be "from news correspondence intended for publication in newspapers entitled to second-class mailing privileges." Accredited members must live in the Washington, D.C. area.

Battles over accreditation have been fought between individual applicants and the Standing Committee of Correspondents. It is no wonder. Prestige is certainly a factor, and without accreditation from the press gallery (or one of the other congressional galleries), a journalist may be denied seating at the reserved media table in congressional committee hearing rooms.

Furthermore, only accredited correspondents can call representatives off the House floor from the Speaker's Lobby or call senators off the floor and accompany them to the Presidents Room for interviews. Congressional accommodation of accredited journalists is not altruistic, of course. Writing in *Congress and the News Media,* James White notes, "While Congress assists the press in reporting. . .the press assists congressmen and senators in publicizing their individual activities to the voters back home and to the nation as a whole."

Accreditation carries a less tangible advantage, too. By being near colleagues, a journalist may pick up story tips.

Although Washington correspondents are competitive on certain stories, they share information regularly. Clark Mollenhoff, a Pulitzer Prize-winning Washington correspondent for the *Des Moines Register* who now teaches and freelances, says that during major investigations he regularly consults with other reporters and makes sure to keep up with the stories they write.

The second congressional gallery for print journalists is the periodical gallery. Each of the working spaces there is staffed by two full-time employees. The Executive Committee (the equivalent of the Standing Committee of Correspondents for newspapers) has seven elected members. They serve for two years. In 1981, the members were from *Time, Newsweek, National Journal,* McGraw-Hill, Kiplinger Washington Editors, Bureau of National Affairs and *U.S. News and World Report.* At least 1000 correspondents from over 200 organizations held credentials through the gallery. The variety of publications that have correspondents reflect the diversity in the world of magazines and newsletters. *Dental Survey, National Catholic Reporter* and *Restaurant Business Magazine* share space with the much better-known news weeklies. Members of the periodical gallery have the same privileges as members of the press gallery, and receive similar services from gallery personnel.

The rules governing admission to the gallery are published in the *Congressional Directory.* Key criteria include employment by periodicals "that regularly publish a substantial volume of news material of either general, economic, industrial, technical, cultural or trade character." The periodical must be operated independently of "any government, industry, institution, association or lobbying organization."

The radio-television gallery had about 1000 accredited members in early 1981. The numbers were higher when producers and camera crew members were figured in. Studios are available in the House and Senate sides of the Capitol, as well as in the Rayburn House Office Building. Each of the areas is staffed by five full-time employees. The gallery is ruled by a seven-member Executive Committee elected for two-year terms. In 1981, the members represented CBS, NBC and ABC news, National Public Radio, Mutual News, Capitol News Reports and Evening News Broadcasting. Each gallery (House and Senate) enforces policies about where correspondents can and cannot film in and around the Capitol and adjacent buildings. The gallery also screens applications from broadcast journalists wishing to cover special events such as the inauguration of the president. To gain accreditation to the gallery, an applicant must earn at least one-half of his income from reporting for broadcast outlets.

The press photographers gallery has three full-time employees to serve the approximately 210 members. The gallery is limited to still photographers; film photographers belong to the radio-television gallery. There is a photo studio in the Dirksen Senate Office Building. A six-member, elected Standing Committee of Press Photographers rules the gallery. The members serve two-year terms. Associated Press Photos is guaranteed one slot on the Standing Committee, as is United Press International Newspictures. One member must represent a magazine (in 1981 that was *Time*) and one member must represent a local newspaper (in 1981 that was the *Washington Post*). The other two members are elected at-large—(in 1981 they represented Associated Press Photos and *Newsweek*). Rules governing admission to the gallery are printed in the *Congressional Directory*.

Accreditation from the Congressional galleries is recognized almost anywhere else in Washington where media credentials are required, but some journalists find it useful to obtain additional accreditation from the White House, State Department, Defense Department or other federal entities. With or without accreditation, however, an investigator can learn plenty about members of Congress and their staffs.

The People on Capitol Hill

Members of Congress all have backgrounds that may hold the key to their behavior. The *Almanac of American Politics,*

Who's Who in American Politics, the *Congressional Directory* and publications from Political Profiles Inc. are good places to begin investigating. Aggregate characteristics of members help show how an individual member is typical or atypical. According to *Congressional Quarterly Weekly Report,* the average age of House members in 1981 was forty-eight, of senators, fifty-three. The most common occupation was lawyer—194 in the House, fifty-nine in the Senate. Other occupations were heavily represented, including business, banking and education. About ninety-six percent were males. Religious affiliation can determine a member's vote on issues like abortion. Roman Catholics were represented more heavily in Congress than were members of any other church.

Personal traits, though not easily quantified, may be important, too. *Washington Post* reporter T.R. Reid understood this when researching articles (and eventually a book called *Congressional Odyssey)* which traced the progress of one bill through Congress. The bill, which proposed charging barge operators for using inland waterways, was sponsored by Senator Pete Domenici, a New Mexico Republican. For several years, Domenici fought against seemingly insurmountable odds. By delving into the senator's character, Reid was able to explain Domenici's persistence. "The senator brought two formidable assets to his uphill fight," Reid reported. "First, Domenici's easygoing manner concealed a tenacious determination to succeed at anything he tried. . .Second. . .Domenici had a strategy."

An investigator who has information about a congressman's family may be able to determine whether the family is helping or hurting the congressman's effectiveness in office. A spouse might run the member's office as an unpaid assistant. Marvella Bayh revealed in her autobiography *Marvella* the open warfare between herself and her husband's Senate staff when she tried to participate. An anti-nepotism law prevents congressmen from hiring their spouses or close relatives; there is no law, however, preventing members from hiring relatives of other members. In his memoirs, House doorkeeper William

"Fishbait" Miller told of relatives on other members' payrolls—one child of a Missouri congressman worked for a California member and a second child was employed by an Ohio member. And there is nothing to prohibit a member and a spouse from both working for the federal government in positions where they can aid each other. In 1980, an Iowa congressman who sat on the Agriculture Committee was married to a high-ranking Agriculture Department official.

The activities of relatives may affect the member of Congress. The legislative work of Senator Thomas Eagleton, already complicated by a tough race for re-election, was affected further in 1980 when his niece was accused of trying to extort $220,000 by threatening to disclose allegedly damaging personal information about him. Reporters Roy Malone and Louis Rose at the *St. Louis Post-Dispatch* used Senate financial records in their investigation of the case. Eagleton took time out from his legislating and campaigning to testify against his niece. She was convicted.

Personal Finances

The Eagleton affair involved a family business. An investigator wanting to learn about a congressman's finances, including a family business, should look at financial disclosure reports filed every May with the clerk of the House or secretary of the Senate. The disclosure reports itemize assets and earnings, including income from outside employment, speaking fees, stock dividends, real estate and gifts.

Clark Mollenhoff observes that "close scrutiny of property acquisitions, living style and payrolls will consistently turn up minor and major abuses of congressional authority." A few congressmen released personal financial information voluntarily before they were required to in 1978. Today, some members disclose more information than is mandated. The *Milwaukee Journal* receives voluntary detailed disclosures from the Wisconsin delegation. Some publish voluntary disclosures in the *Congressional Record*, including otherwise confidential tax payments. The 1980 voluntary statement of

Representative Richard Ottinger, a New York Democrat, showed assets of almost $2 million, mostly stocks and bonds. Ot-
tinger revealed that he paid federal income tax of $70,000,
state and local income taxes of $20,000 and property taxes
totalling $6000.

Unfortunately, disclosure categories on the mandatory
forms are broad. A member with unearned income of $1 million
could use the category "over $100,000." *Congressional
Quarterly Weekly Report* said that one wealthy congressman
listed his holdings in a private corporation as "over $250,000,"
the highest category. But at market value, those holdings were
worth more than $16 million.

Audits of senators' statements by the General Accounting
Office have shown inaccuracies. Nonetheless, for an investigator the forms are a starting place. From them, he could
learn that Representative Dan Rostenkowski, an Illinois
Democrat, topped the House in 1979 by collecting over $29,000
in honoraria for speeches. Because the House had placed a
limit on outside earned income, including honoraria,
Rostenkowski could keep only about $9000. The remainder he
had to donate to charity. In the Senate, Henry Jackson, a
Washington Democrat, topped the honoraria list with nearly
$31,000. The limit was $25,000, so Jackson, like Rostenkowski,
had to give away some of the money. Who paid these
honoraria? The Grocery Manufacturers of America led all
organizations, spending nearly $27,000 in 1979.

An investigator might use the forms to examine speaking
fees from specific industries and relate them to a member's
votes on legislation affecting those industries. When Iowa
Senator John Culver accepted $3500 in speaking fees from the
billboard industry while his committee was considering
billboard legislation, William Symonds of the *Des Moines
Register* raised questions in a thoroughly researched article.
The disclosure forms may suggest other conflicts of interests to
an investigator—when one-third of House Agriculture Committee members own farms, can they be objective voting on federal
farm policies? When a congressman owns stock in Chrysler

Corporation, should he be voting on federal loan guarantees for that firm?

Income from second jobs raises questions as well. The 1980 reports revealed that thirty-five senators and 153 representatives held part-time jobs, jobs that presumably distracted them from their duties as elected officials.

Campaign Finances

When a member of Congress receives money for a speech, it generally is not meant for use in his re-election campaign. But if money is given to a congressman's authorized campaign committee, it is meant to aid his re-election. Campaign contributions are reported to the Federal Election Commission. Big bucks are involved. The average cost of a Senate campaign is over $1 million; an average House race costs over $200,000—and those figures exclude spending in primary elections. During the 1979-80 election cycle, candidates for the 435 House seats spent about $130 million. Candidates for one-third of the Senate seats spent about $100 million.

By reading reports at the FEC, an investigator can unearth a tremendous amount of useful information. It helps that FEC records are computerized, allowing an investigator to retrieve data at terminals in the public disclosure room.

Heavy campaign contributions are part of the reason why incumbents tend to win re-election. In the House, usually 90 percent of all incumbents running in the general election are victorious. The Senate figure hovers around 70 percent. In 1980, despite the media's focus on some startling upsets, incumbents in fact fared well in the general election. Just thirty-seven of 410 House incumbents who ran were losers. Over 70 percent of the incumbents received at least 60 percent of the vote—landslide proportions. In the Senate, twenty-one of twenty-nine incumbents won.

Incumbents almost always raise more money than their challengers. The support comes from individuals, political parties and political action committees established by corporations, unions and other organizations. Comparing an incumbent's contributors with those of a challenger might lead an investigator to ask which candidate is receiving more money in small donations from individuals. Do those donations reflect grassroots support? How much money is coming from outside the district or state? Is the incumbent accepting contributions from organizations with a special interest in the congressional committees on which he serves? Is there a favor expected in return? How much financial support is coming from the candidate's political party?

"[Campaign finance] reports can provide investigative reporters with a valuable leg up," said Pat Riordan of the *Miami Herald* in the *Investigative Reporters and Editors Journal.* "They tell you who supports your candidate. They show his special interest backing. They report out-of-state money. And they're publicly available today as never before."

Every candidate's authorized campaign committee has a treasurer who is a potential source; if the treasurer is a prominent person, that fact might be interesting in itself. Many treasurers are not sophisticated Washington types, and therefore are more likely to talk about ongoing FEC investigations or other sensitive matters. (Files of FEC investigations, called "matters under review," are public record, but only after the case is closed.) Rumors alleging a person's candidacy can be verified by looking to see whether that person has designated an authorized committee at the FEC. By law, a person becomes a candidate after receiving contributions or making expenditures of $5000. Once a candidacy is triggered, the candidate has fifteen days to designate a committee.

The committee treasurer must keep a record of every contribution over $50. The name, address, occupation and principal place of business for every contributor giving over $200 in a calendar year must be disclosed to the FEC. Individuals and political committees are limited by law to a maximum amount of giving per candidate per election.

Reports by campaign committees can be filed at any time, but the main filing deadlines occur six times during an election year. Quarterly reports are due April 15, July 15 and October

15; pre-election reports are due twelve days before a primary and twelve days before a general election; and a post-election report is due thirty days after the general election. The year-end report detailing committee receipts and expenditures is due January 31 of the following year. During non-election years, reports are filed less frequently.

As of 1981, candidates for Congress had to raise their own money; no public funding was available (in contrast to presidential campaigns). Besides a candidate's authorized committee, other committees—usually not identified with just one candidate—are major factors in campaign finances. They, too, must file reports at the FEC. Some are affiliated with political parties. The committees receiving the most attention, however, are formally called "non-party, non-candidate committees," or "political action committees (PACs)." They are established by businesses, unions, trade associations and ideological groups for the express purpose of contributing to candidates. One type of PAC written about often in 1980 was the ideological group spending money to benefit a candidate, sometimes independently of the candidate's own organization. A few of these groups were liberal, but the wealthiest, most visible ones were conservative. *Business Week* noted that the National Conservative Political Action Committee raised $5 million in 1980 in its effort to unseat liberal Democrats. The largest liberal PAC, the National Committee for an Effective Congress, raised one-fourth that amount.

By combining campaign reports from various sources, an investigator can convey an overall picture. A *Wall Street Journal* profile of Archer-Daniels-Midland Co. disclosed not only how the corporate PAC gave generously to certain candidates, but also that the company's chairman and members of his family had contributed generously as individuals. Common Cause specializes in linking contributions from special interests to incumbents' votes on issues of vital concern to those groups.

Not just anyone can help in a candidate's campaign, however. An incumbent has a personal staff—and sometimes committee staffers—who are vitally interested in his re-election. The challenger has no such staff. Because congressional aides are paid with taxpayer dollars, there are informal restrictions on their use in campaigns, although there is little consensus on specifics. A 1980 Senate guidebook says if a staffer "is to participate to a great extent in the re-election campaign of a member of Congress, removing that staff employee from the official congressional payroll and paying him a salary from campaign accounts has been recommended. Such a procedure may be used as a method for avoiding the problems of distinguishing between the 'official' time and the 'free' time of the staffer, and eliminating the problem of attempting to distinguish between the 'official political' duties of the staffer as opposed to merely 'political campaign' activities directed solely toward the member's re-election."

But a 1981 *New York Times* article on the subject cited a just-released federal appeals court opinion which dismissed a suit claiming that a senator had broken the law by keeping his administrative assistant on the Senate payroll while the aide was spending long hours campaigning for the senator's re-election. *Times* reporter Stuart Taylor Jr. noted the implications of the ruling; there would be no legal restrictions on the use of aides in political campaigns unless Congress chose to create them.

An investigator examining campaign finances is wise to be on the lookout for similar extraordinary uses of staff by members of Congress. He should also be aware of prohibitions, under certain conditions, against help from executive branch civil servants, foreign nationals and government contractors.

One type of fundraising by members of Congress is so typical that it deserves special attention by Washington investigators. It is the Washington testimonial. Jerry Landauer, an investigative reporter for the *Wall Street Journal*, noted, in a 1980 article, that on any one day as many as a dozen incumbents and challengers might be competing for attention—and money—at receptions, dinners or lunches.

"If the prospective donor wants to conclude that he is purchasing legislative favors, that obviously is his own doing,"

Landauer said. "What politicians mostly hold up for sale is the alluring possibility of influence, rather than the real thing." On just one day in 1980 the *Washington Post* style section contained three full-length stories on congressional fundraisers: one for Republican House challenger Newton Steers at the home of House Minority Leader John Rhodes, one for New Jersey Democratic Representative Frank Thompson at a downtown hotel, and one for Florida Democratic Representative Claude Pepper at the home of lobbyist Thomas Corcoran.

Tracking money raised at these events by reading FEC reports is difficult, because of loopholes in the disclosure requirements. So an investigator must be alert, hearing of them by word of mouth, or checking with the House and Senate Democratic and Republican campaign committees which usually keep track of such events. The fundraising galas often yield good stories: A Nevada congressman evokes the Wild West by serving an annual banquet of buffalo, quail and venison to his contributors; a Florida congressman with Ringling Brothers and Barnum & Bailey circus in his district includes an evening with circus performers in the price of the ticket to his annual fundraiser in Washington, D.C. But colorful fundraisers can also lead to serious stories about big money and its influence on legislation (a senior member of Congress can take in between $15,000 and $60,000 during the evening). Sometimes lobbyists sponsor the fundraisers, even doing the organizational work. They and others who attend are usually vitally interested in how the member votes. For example, a Washington fundraiser for Representative Joseph Addabbo, a New York Democrat, was attended by defense contractors. Addabbo was chairman of the House Appropriations subcommittee on defense. The assistant treasurer for the event was James McDonald, a lobbyist for Northrop Corp., a defense contractor. More than $23,000 worth of tickets were sold. John Murphy, a New York Democratic congressman, threw a fundraiser in Washington while the committee he chaired, Merchant Marine and Fisheries, was drafting a reform of maritime law. Maritime groups attended in large numbers. The take: nearly $65,000, according to *Congressional Quarterly Weekly Report.*

Congressional Pay and Privileges

The annual salary of each member of Congress was $60,662 in 1981. The speaker of the House and the Senate president pro tem, majority leader and minority leader received extra amounts. Even when a member loses, he is set for life financially. When fifty-three-year-old John Brademas, an Indiana Democrat, was defeated in 1980 after serving eleven House terms, he was guaranteed an annual pension of at least $31,000, according to a *Wall Street Journal* inquiry.

Allowances for official expenses are generous. In 1981, an average House member received about $575,000 of taxpayer funds to carry out his duties. The Senate figure ranged from roughly $750,000 to $1.5 million, depending on the population of the state represented. The bulk of these sums goes for staff salaries, but, especially in the House, "official expenses" can mean almost anything. A 1980 *Washington Post* article noted these examples: A California House office spent over $2700 on lunches for visitors to Washington; dozens of members kept leased cars in their districts; a Kentucky member spent over $1000 during 1979 on sympathy cards for the bereaved in his district.

Looking through the expense records was "not unlike tripping through a great mail-order catalog of life's amenities," said Ward Sinclair of the *Post.* "If it exists, it's almost certain that a member of the House bought it—under the rubric of 'official' purpose, of course."

The base House allowance for official expenses was $43,000 per member in 1981, but the average amount spent was probably twice that. Travel to and from the district was paid for from a separate fund, with reimbursement by the mile. Long-distance telephone calls and rent for district offices came from still other funds. Each member received an additional sum for purchasing electrical and mechanical office equipment. Newsletters to constituents, questionnaires about current issues and radio and television tapes produced in Capitol Hill studios—all are subsidized by taxpayers' money.

In 1979, members of Congress spent $42 million on franked mail, according to the Postal Service. The House Commission on Congressional Mailing Standards has published a sixty-page book explaining the complex do's and don'ts of sending mail for free. The Senate published a separate guide. The volume of free mass mailings to the district tends to rise every other year as the primaries and the November elections approach.

Senate office expense accounts ranged from $33,000 to $143,000 in 1981. Senators and their employees cannot use office accounts for such things as entertaining visitors or leasing cars back home all year-round.

Many of the day-to-day expenditures of taxpayers' dollars are compiled in the quarterly report of the clerk of the House and in the semi-annual report of the secretary of the Senate. The thick books are difficult to read, but in them the persistent investigator will find a wealth of information on expenditures of individual members, their employees, House and Senate committees and congressional support arms.

Jockeying for office space is part of the congressional ritual. In the Senate, seniority is a factor, but space in the office buildings is assigned according to a state's population, with members from bigger states generally getting more rooms because of their larger staffs. No matter who the senator, furnishings are supplied—including an unabridged dictionary with its own stand. Priority House office building assignments go to members with the longest continuous service. New members draw numbers to determine the order of selection for remaining suites. Basic furnishings are provided including pictures for the walls and custom framing; potted plants are available from the congressional botanic gardens.

Patronage is yet another privilege. In the House, it is doled out by the Committee on Personnel of the majority party; the minority party receives little. Available positions include those as pages, doormen, elevator operators, mail clerks and more. In the Senate, patronage is controlled by the Democratic Caucus and the Republican Personnel Committee. Every House and Senate member can make nominations to the military academies; senators play a major role in selecting federal judges for their own states.

As privileges go, patronage is peanuts compared to foreign travel (unkindly referred to as "junketing"). In 1979, nearly 300 members of Congress reported 536 trips abroad at government expense. The amount of money spent on those trips topped $2.4 million, according to "official" figures published in the *Congressional Record*. But *Congressional Quarterly Weekly Report* determined the true total was about $4.5 million. The higher amount included costs absorbed by the Defense Department and other agencies for air transportation and escort officers. *Congressional Quarterly's* method of investigation is instructive. First, the magazine asked each member to list every foreign country visited in 1979, the dates and purposes of each trip, and at whose expense the trip was taken. Second, the magazine collected committee and delegation reports published from time to time in the *Congressional Record*. Third, files were examined at the Army, Navy, Air Force and State departments. Fourth, the magazine surveyed foreign trips paid for by private groups. Trips of that kind valued at over $250 must be disclosed on the personal financial forms described earlier in this chapter.

An investigator wishing to determine the foreign travel of just one congressman can use *Congressional Quarterly* as a starting point; once a year the magazine publishes a member-by-member breakdown. An investigator should be aware of nuances—sometimes spouses and children accompany the member of Congress, but what they pay may be far below the true cost to the government. Many of the trips are justifiable, of course. Investigators need to evaluate them on a case-by-case basis.

An investigator should not ignore domestic travel made at taxpayer expense. As recently as 1960, members were authorized only three trips home each year at government expense. By 1981 the number had increased more than tenfold. Such allowances make it easier for a member to go back to the district often, which may or may not be desirable, depending on one's philosophy of government. Richard Fenno Jr., a political scientist, found that the average annual number of trips home—not counting recesses—was thirty-five. Almost one-third of the House members surveyed returned to their districts every weekend.

Personal Staff as Privilege

Perhaps the most important privilege a member of Congress enjoys is the ability to hire a personal staff at public expense. (Some members, especially committee and subcommittee chairmen and ranking minority members, also have the right to handpick staffers for committee work. Although personal staffers perform different duties and have different loyalties than committee staffers, the distinction between them can be hazy, especially in the Senate.)

The growth of congressional staff has been a topic of debate for at least the past decade. Since staffers are paid with tax dollars, it is legitimate for an investigator to compare a congressman's staffing costs with those of other members, or with those of the same congressman ten or twenty years earlier. Many congressmen will reveal staff salaries on request; if a member does not cooperate, an investigator can almost always piece together salaries from clerk of the House and secretary of the Senate reports, though that is difficult because the reports do not coincide with calendar years. Other expenses attributable to staff, including their domestic and foreign travel, can be located in these reports unless concealment is being practiced by a congressman. In 1980, after studying secretary of the Senate reports and other documents, a UPI reporter moved a story revealing that at least 160 staff aides in the Senate received salaries above $50,000 a year.

There are limits on the total a member can spend for staff salaries in a year, and limits on how much any one personal staffer can be paid. As of 1981 in the House, a member's total staff salary allowance was $336,000; the individual maximum was slightly over $50,000. There are limits, too, on how many personal staffers a representative can have. In 1981, that limit was twenty-two.

In the Senate, the payment ceiling depends on the population of the state represented. The 1981 range for the "administrative and clerical assistance allowance" was $593,000 to $1,191,000. The ceiling on individual salaries was about $53,000. Unlike representatives, senators can hire as many staffers as they want as long as they do not top the overall salary ceiling; some senators hire extra staff at their own expense. A study found one senator with fourteen personal staffers, another with seventy. Senators in 1981 received an additional $184,000 for hiring legislative assistants to handle specific issues; these issues usually relate to a senator's committee assignments. Committee chairmen and the ranking minority member received less than the full $184,000 because of the right they have to handpick committee staffers who are answerable only to them.

The salaries of personal staffers might be of occasional interest, but it is what the staffers do every day that makes for a continuing story. Much of their work is quasi-political; their goal, usually unspoken, is to make sure their employer is not defeated at the polls. That means responding to the needs of constituents. Almost every congressman keeps personal staff back home to deal with constituents face-to-face. The office space back home, including mobile offices, is generally paid for with public funds.

The average representative has two offices in his district; the average senator has three in the state. Challengers complain that district offices are little more than taxpayer-financed campaign headquarters. *Congressional Quarterly Weekly Report*, in a 1981 article, reported about 2500 district staffers, more than double the amount a decade earlier. To learn what is on constituents' minds, an investigator can look at the casework files in a congressman's Washington and district offices. Many problems concern Social Security, veterans' benefits and military service. Others may be localized to a member's district or state. Much of the mail (over 55 million pieces to Congress in 1980) is not strictly casework—constituents write in wanting to know a congressman's position on abortion, defense spending or some other issue. However mundane responding to constituent mail and visits may seem, it takes up the bulk of the day for many personal staffers and sometimes for the member of Congress himself.

If a congressman runs for re-election on the platform of good constituent service, it is legitimate to ask whether the legislating function has been ignored. It is certainly legitimate to question how well the member's office performed its casework, or whether "personal" communication with constituents at taxpayer expense was worth the money. When every nurse in the district receives a computer-generated "personal" letter that includes a *Congressional Record* reprint on how the member voted to increase funding for nurses' training, how personal is the letter? An investigator could point out that the costs of the computer and the reprint were borne by the taxpayers. (James Pates, a former Hill staffer, wrote in the *Fredericksburg (Virginia) Free Lance-Star* that sophisticated members of Congress "use their computers to compile hundreds of lists. The file on each individual often amounts to a veritable portrait," including data on age, sex, race, occupation and political party.) When a congressman sends a questionnaire—drafted by his staff—to constituents, does it matter that the response is unscientific, that the questions may have been loaded?

Who are these staffers who influence a congressman's thinking, who run his office in ways advantageous to his re-election? Most staffers are intensely loyal to their boss. Some have worked in his election campaign; others have grown up in his state or district. Almost all professional staffers are college-educated; many have advanced degrees. Legislative assistants may be specialists by training, especially in the Senate. The administrative assistant, usually the member's right-hand man or woman, tends to be a generalist attuned to the politics back home.

The press secretary is a key staffer and the person an investigator should probably call on when trying to contact a member of Congress for the first time. The press secretary's main job is to get the boss's name in the news. But the press secretary can direct an investigator to the staffer who can provide the most information, or convince the member to carve out time for an interview. Some press secretaries have a journalistic background, some do not. Of those who do, most are former print reporters, although there is a significant minority of former broadcasters.

Personal staffers sometimes are more than just hand-maidens who aid in the re-election of their employers. William Safire, *New York Times* columnist, told of regular meetings in 1980 of the Madison Group, a dozen or so hawkish, conservative, mostly Senate staffers. "Most of the time, the Madison Group operated as a separate focus of power, with the staffers' senators not fully knowing—or wanting to know—what their employees were doing," Safire said.

Congressional staffers have their own organizations, such as the Senate Association of Administrative Assistants and Secretaries or the Association of House Democratic Press Assistants. They also have their own publication, *Staff: Congressional Staff Journal,* which like most publications written by insiders for insiders, tends to be revealing. In 1981, it was published six times a year by the Committee on House Administration.

The Member of Congress as Legislator

Every piece of legislation pushed or opposed by a member, every vote in committee and on the floor, can be viewed in two contexts by an investigator. The first is how it will affect the member's chances for re-election. The second is how it will help him achieve his policy objectives.

Each bill introduced in the House or Senate has a primary sponsor, and many carry the names of cosponsors. Every day, the *Congressional Record* runs a list of bills introduced. Sponsorship may be significant—although numerous congressional insiders say privately that most bills are introduced for show. An investigator can ask around to learn whether a sponsor really believes in his proposal, or whether it was introduced for political or symbolic reasons. In *Senator*, Washington correspondent Elizabeth Drew said of one senator: "He does not take on a large number of issues, and those that he takes on tend to be ones that make an important point—and also ones on which he feels he has a reasonable chance of winning." He is contrasted with another senator, of whom it is said, "If twenty-five of the fifty bills he introduced were never heard of again, he didn't give it another thought."

Some bills are identical to those introduced previously. In such instances, the most recent sponsor may be trying to gain credit without doing his own work. A few congressmen will try to gain credit by deliberately confusing cosponsorship with sponsorship in a news release. A bill's true sponsor may solicit cosponsors in large numbers. Or he may ask only influential colleagues, hoping that having their names attached to the bill will help it through the legislative maze. Committee or subcommittee chairmen may line up cosponsors on their committee or subcommittee to signal that the bill probably will emerge for consideration on the floor. Members often circulate "dear colleague" letters to attract cosponsors. The letters are an important means of internal communication, and often provide timely, useful summaries of legislation.

Too rarely do investigators determine why a member sponsored a bill—it is not always because he strongly supports the proposal. James Deakin of the *St. Louis Post-Dispatch* said when covering legislation, "I try to determine whether a member of Congress needed the support of someone like the postal unions or the coal miners in his district to get here and stay here. This can be more revealing of how he will act than anything else." Comparing the bills introduced with a member's campaign contributors can be fruitful. Concentrated special-interest support for a bill might be unwittingly revealed by the sponsor himself through publication of support letters in the *Congressional*

Record. A look at who cared enough to write those letters might yield interesting leads.

Even the busiest senators with national reputations will champion seemingly inconsequential bills because of back-home special interests. One instance was detailed in a 1980 *New York Times* story by A.O. Sulzberger Jr. about the battle over whether car bumpers should be steel or aluminum. A large manufacturer of steel bumpers was in West Virginia, home state of then Senate Majority Leader Robert Byrd. The aluminum industry was a major employer in Washington state, home of Warren Magnuson, then Senate Appropriations Committee chairman. Byrd and Magnuson were fighting over whether car bumpers should be able to withstand impacts of 5 or 2½ miles per hour.

An investigator should remember that relatively few bills become law, no matter who the sponsor. Tracing the history of a Senate bill, T.R. Reid of the *Washington Post* noted the Senate rarely considers more than ten a week, and sometimes takes ten weeks to act on one bill. Most die in committee without consideration—only about 10 percent get a hearing. The fact is, many bills are never intended to go anywhere. Introducing legislation "is a no-lose proposition," Reid said. "By sponsoring a bill that's important to some constituent or pressure group, the member can honestly say that he or she has done the group a favor." Opposing groups are unlikely to become alarmed, because so many bills are dropped into the hopper any week. In the 96th Congress (1979-80), over 10,000 measures were introduced in the House, but only about 1400 were approved. In the Senate, about the same number passed, of 4100 introduced. And some bills approved in one chamber died in the other—only 613 public bills were signed into law. Some bills kick around for years before they pass. Former Louisiana Congressman F. Edward Hebert first proposed legislation to create an armed services medical school in the early 1940s. Year after year, Hebert reintroduced it, with no success. It was not until the 1970s, after Hebert became chairman of the House Armed Services Committee, that the university became a reality.

Looking at final passage is not enough for an investigator trying to gauge a member's success rate. Some congressmen are masters at guiding bills or amendments through subcommittee and committee—where the spotlight shines dimly, if at all.

The nature of the legislation a congressman introduces, combined with the committee assignments he seeks, may reveal whether he perceives himself mainly as a national policymaker or as a pusher of special projects for folks back home. Some members fit equally well into both categories. Louisiana Democratic Senator Russell Long chaired the Finance Committee in 1980, and thus controlled tax matters vital to everyone. But, in a *Washington Post* profile during Long's 1980 re-election campaign, the reporter illustrated how Long reminded constituents about the billions of dollars he had brought back to Louisiana—an auto plant for Shreveport, a World's Fair for New Orleans and $3 billion annually from oil and gas decontrol.

Often congressmen try to help constituents through committee assignments. Members with military bases in their districts are better able to halt cutbacks at the bases—and maybe successfully push for expansion—if they sit on the Armed Services Committee. Of course, some congressmen seek seats on the Armed Services Committee in order to influence military policy. They may care little about direct benefits to their districts—or may not even have bases in their districts at all. But one study, *Congress and the Bureaucracy* by R. Douglas Arnold, showed that during the 1960s and 1970s, the Armed Services Committee attracted a disproportionate number of congressmen with installations in their area.

Appropriations Committee members can exercise vast influence on national policy by deciding how much money to allocate to new or continuing programs. Appropriations Committee members use their positions, too, to obtain specific benefits. Arnold said that when the Department of Housing and Urban Development selected 150 municipalities for funding under the Model Cities Program, none was in the district of Appropriations Committee member Representative Joseph McDade, a Pennsylvania Republican. During hearings, McDade hammered away at the bureaucrats, wondering what was so sacrosanct about the number 150. He was not advocating a major expansion of the program. He wanted his district to share in the benefits. Not long after, Scranton—in McDade's district—became the 151st model city.

Another way members fight for localized benefits is by tinkering with allocations of money. Thus, a New England senator will offer a seemingly innocuous amendment making "degree heat days" a criterion for heating oil aid to low-income persons. In effect, the senator is trying to take part of the allocation from another region and channel it to his. Spencer Rich of the *Washington Post* wrote about this technique, in a front-page article. The formula game hides "a grubby reality," Rich said. "The formula that seemed fairest and most equitable to each senator usually turned out to be the formula that helped his state to a bigger slice of the pie."

A congressman's committee selections can be viewed as part of a national pattern (which regions are most heavily represented on which committees, and why) or through a more localized perspective. Each member jockeys furiously for a seat on his preferred committees at the start of each Congress. Some committees have more requests for assignment than they have openings. If the member is successful, what does that mean for his constituents? If he is unsuccessful, will that hurt his district or state?

Democrats and Republicans in each chamber have their own procedures for assigning congressmen to committees. In the House, for example, the Democratic Steering and Policy Committee, with twenty-nine members in 1981, played an influential role. The party in control has claim to every chairmanship and writes the chamber's rules, including the proportion of Democrats to Republicans on each committee. The committee ratio was hotly debated in the House during 1981; Democrats decreed two-to-one ratios on several vital committees, even though their party controlled just 56 percent of House seats.

A continuing saga is how every member of Congress, whatever his committee assignments, claws to carve out a unique specialty. The specialty is usually related to the committees on which the member serves (especially in the House), and may or may not relate directly to the interests of the member's district. Sometimes a member is blocked by a congressman with more senority who already is recognized as the expert on a particular issue.

Some committee assignments turn out to be more symbolic than substantive. Certain members of Congress do little on a committee to which they have been assigned. In part, that is due to circumstances beyond the control of members. In 1980, the average representative sat on six committees or subcommittees. The average senator sat on ten. The House Small Business Committee, for example, was perceived (rightly or wrongly) as a "re-election" committee, meaning many members postured frequently to gain the support of small business people but otherwise devoted little time to the problems of small business.

In addition to their work on the well-known standing committees, many congressmen serve on special panels or join special-interest caucuses within Congress. Their activity (or non-activity) within such groups is noteworthy. A 1980 *National Journal* story told of one active caucus, the fifty-five-member Suburban Caucus, and its fight to reverse an executive branch policy that encouraged federal offices to locate in central business districts.

The proliferation of caucuses in recent years has been rapid. A count in 1980 revealed forty of them. In early 1981, the *Washington Post* told about the formation of yet another—the House Arts Caucus. A few caucuses are partisan, but most cut across party lines. Many are based in the House, though there are several based in the Senate; a number are bicameral. The House Office of Records and Registration has reports of receipts and expenditures on file from some caucuses. The receipts column can indicate strong ties to lobbying groups.

A 1981 story by Jerry Landauer in the *Wall Street Journal* raised the question of whether the Travel and Tourism Caucus was a government-supported lobby. For instance, when the Travel and Tourism Caucus held a $250-a-plate dinner that net-ted $175,000, many of the 700 attendees were from the travel and tourism industry. The caucus has its own space in a House office building and a full-time staff. (About half the caucuses had paid staff, according to a 1979 study.) Nearly half the members of Congress had joined it as of 1981. It takes stands on issues, sometimes after listening to an advisory board consisting of several dozen industry leaders—for example, the president of the Recreational Vehicle Industry Association.

In addition to the caucuses, there are other unusual or temporary bodies on which a member of Congress can serve. For instance, in 1980 the chairman of the House Armed Services Committee named Representative Bob Carr, a Michigan Democrat, to head a special panel within the committee. The panel was to recommend ways of improving the readiness of the armed forces, focusing on weapons already in hand: Carr had been complaining that the Pentagon concentrates too much on buying new weapons and too little on keeping current weapons in fighting condition.

A quick look through the 1980 *Congressional Directory* turned up, for example, bodies like the National Commission on Unemployment Compensation, with seven persons appointed by the president, three by the Senate and three by the House. One member was a congressman. The organization had a budget and a professional staff. What did it do? Was it making good use of taxpayers' dollars? Who in the Senate and House appointed the private citizen members? How were these members selected—on the basis of expertise, or as a political payoff? The eighteen-member Japan-United States Friendship Commission, chaired by a Yale University professor, included four members of Congress in addition to a newspaper editor and an assistant secretary of state. What did it do?

Other peripheral but useful ways of thinking about congressmen as legislators include:

• Members as part of a state delegation. Congressmen from the same state may have a great deal in common, especially when it comes to public works projects, general revenue sharing and other non-partisan matters. Senior members of a state delegation often work hard to obtain desired committee assignments for freshmen. In at least a few states, there is dissension, with members working at cross-purposes. Some state delegations meet regularly, often over breakfast. Reporters can sometimes gain access to these meetings. Clark Mollenhoff, author of *Investigative Reporting,* says he made a point of developing sources in the Iowa delegation during the twenty-eight years he reported for the *Des Moines Register* in Washington. "On almost any investigative effort, the reporter must have allies in obtaining information that's not readily available from public sources," he said. Members of Congress often succeed in unearthing information from federal agencies where private investigators fail. Committees on which a member of Congress serves can threaten to subpoena documents, if informal requests have been in vain.

• Members' voting records. Dozens of groups in the private sector, from the U.S. Chamber of Commerce to the Americans for Democratic Action, publish vote ratings of congressmen. Ratings do have pitfalls. Nevertheless, looking at how a congressmen is rated can provide a sense of his liberal—or conservative—nature. Furthermore, ratings often indicate how much campaign support members of Congress will receive from special interests. An investigator examining a congressman's voting record should study votes in committee, not just roll call votes on the floor. Yet almost nobody ever delves into a member's committee voting record to see whether it differs either from public statements or from later floor votes. *Congressional Quarterly Weekly Report* compiles attendance at roll call votes on the House and Senate floors for every member every year. In an extreme case, Massachusetts Senator Edward Kennedy missed 82 percent of floor votes during 1980, partly because of his bid for the Democratic presidential nomination. Investigators can piece together up-to-date attendance figures using the *Congressional Record. Congressional Quarterly* complies additional voting studies of each member. They include support of the president's legislative initiatives; measures of party unity on floor votes; and the relative strength or weakness of the conservative coalition. The percentages sometimes dispel textbook descriptions of Congress. For example, party unity scores indicate that the majority of House Democrats is united against the majority of Republicans on far less than half of all votes.

• Members and conflicts of interests. Disclosure of personal finances and holdings was meant to eliminate conflict-of-interests problems. But disclosure is at most a band-aid solution. Frequently a member will still vote in committee or on the floor if legislation will benefit him or his family. An investigation by Tracy Freedman of *Washington Journalism Review* turned up forty members of Congress who owned stock in media companies. At the time of the investigation, Freedman found ninety-seven media-related bills pending. "Will the forty congressmen with media holdings abstain from voting for fear of conflict of interest?" Freedman asked. "Probably not," she answered. What about a congressman representing a district dependent on coal when he is a stockholder in a coal mining company? It can be argued that the congressman's holdings require him to abstain. But it can be argued just as forcefully that abstaining would deprive his constituents of representation on a matter vital to them. There are Senate and House rules on conflict of interests. The wording is strong, as in this section of the Senate rule: "No member. . .shall knowingly use his official position to introduce or aid the progress or passage of legislation, a principal purpose of which is to further only his pecuniary interest, only the pecuniary interest of his immediate family, or only the pecuniary interest of a limited class of persons or enterprises when he or his immediate family or enterprises controlled by them are members of the affected class." Yet what all those words boil down to is "let your conscience be your guide." In 1979, *Congressional Quarterly* counted at least fifty-four senators and 105 representatives with conflicts between their own holdings and their committee assignments. Another potential voting conflict occurs when members receive sizable campaign contributions from special-interest groups. An industrious investigator might be able to determine vote-buying; if not that, he might be able to establish a pattern of voting by the member that is in accord with a special interest's goals.

• Members as part of the congressional leadership. Not all members can be part of the leadership, of course. Not all want to be. But if a senior congressman is not part of the leadership, a look at why could be productive. Reputations mean a lot. Is the member an outsider in his chamber? Writing for the New Yorker, respected Washington journalist Elizabeth Drew said of senators: "Some become known as mediocrities, some as well-meaning but ineffective, some as phonies, some as mavericks. . .a few are dismissed as jokes, and a few are taken seriously." In the House, the majority party leadership includes the speaker, majority whip, chief deputy whip, deputy whips, at-large whips, zone whips, chairman of the Democratic Caucus, members of the Steering and Policy Committee and chairman of the Democratic Congressional Campaign Committee. House Republicans and each party in the Senate have their leadership members, too. The leaders can focus attention on issues when they choose to. The House speaker holds briefings before Congress convenes each day. During 1980, Saturday morning news conferences by the Senate majority leader usually resulted in Sunday headlines.

The Workings of Committees and Subcommittees

Every piece of legislation introduced in the House or the Senate is referred to a committee. Internal rules determine which bill goes to what committee. In the House a 1980 count indicated there were eighteen committees and sixty-five subcommittees with some jurisdiction over energy. Because some bills may be handled by more than one committee, the jockeying by a bill's sponsor to have it referred to a certain committee, rather than another with similar jurisdiction, can be a story in itself. T.R. Reid wrote in Congressional Odyssey that while following the fate of a bill for the *Washington Post,* he recognized the dilemma of its sponsor, Senator Pete Domenici. Under one logical interpretation, the bill could have been sent to the Finance Committee. But Domenici knew the chairman of that committee was an "implacable foe" of the bill. That same chairman, Senator Russell Long, headed a subcommittee of the Commerce Committee, another panel to which Domenici's bill could logically have been referred. Domenici wanted his bill referred to the congenial Environment and Public Works Committee. But, said Reid, "it was one thing to determine the best committee for the bill to land in; it was something else to arrange for it to land there."

No matter where bills are referred, most never receive committee consideration. Neglect is due to opposition of the chairman, the existence of other pressing matters or simply because the bill was never intended to go anywhere. Furthermore, not all committee hearings center their attention on bills. Investigations to determine whether legislation is necessary also consume a committee's limited time and resources.

Hearings, whether on a particular bill or a general problem, do not always provide an unbiased picture. When the tobacco subcommittee of the House Agriculture Committee held a hearing on the dangers of cigarette smoke to non-smokers, the witnesses were pro-tobacco—it was no surprise; almost all of the subcommittee members were from tobacco-producing regions.

Minority party members can call their own witnesses; those invited to testify by the Democrats and those invited by the Republicans often have philosophical differences. But when committee members, such as those on the tobacco panel, are united by their support of tobacco production, party affiliation becomes secondary. The chairman is often the major force in determining who will testify and who will not. As the rules for one House committee say, "the scheduling of witnesses and the time allowed for the presentation of testimony and interrogation shall be at the sole discretion of the chairman. . .except as otherwise provided in these rules."

A 1980 *Washington Post* story disclosed how one witness list was stacked, intentionally or not. The forum was the House subcommittee for Labor-HEW of the Appropriations Committee. The topic: how much federal money to allocate for diabetes research. Almost every witness wanted more money for research. Publicly they talked about the progess already made and the bright outlook for further advances if only there were enough money. Off-the-record, however, there were pessimistic exchanges between advocates of diabetes research and subcommittee chairman William Natcher, a Kentucky Democrat. Only one witness, Carl Stenzler, questioned the need for ever-expanding research budgets. But, asked *Post* reporter Ward Sinclair, would Congress listen? The likely answer was no. Stenzler's six pages of testimony in the subcommittee hearing record contrasted dramatically with the remaining 5046 pages, which urged that more money be spent.

When a subcommittee hears an apparently objective expert witness—often someone from the academic world—the witness is in truth handpicked by the subcommittee chairman or the sponsor of the bill. Witnesses customarily prepare their testimony in conjunction with the subcommittee staffer who requested it. Hearings are not always spontaneous even when they give that appearance. An investigator might ask who chose certain witnesses and why, whether people seeking to testify were denied, who actually wrote the testimony, whether the questions and answers after the testimony were outlined in advance and whether some witnesses were reimbursed for time and travel while others were not. (Senate rules as of 1981 allowed "summoned" witnesses $75 a day plus transportation expenses.)

Congressional committees are giving increasing attention to "oversight," that is, to determining how effectively laws are being administered. But even though many committees have "oversight" subcommittees, Congress generally does a poor job of systematically monitoring implementation by the bureaucracy. Determining whether public policy is being implemented as Congress intended is perceived as neither exciting nor rewarding at the polls. It is also difficult work—by one count, implementation of a relatively straighforward program like revenue sharing involved fifteen agencies.

When the Senate holds hearings on a presidential nomination to a Cabinet department or regulatory agency, there are elements of oversight. The questions senators ask the nominee often reflect how those senators believe the bureaucracy should perform. Oversight is part of the appropriations process, too. Most federal agencies must come before Congress every year to request money. Appropriations subcommittees in the House and Senate specify the purposes for which dollars can be spent.

If a committee has failed to conduct oversight hearings, what might be suggested—among other things—is an unusually cozy relationship between the subcommittee chairman and certain bureaucrats. It is possible to uncover the relationship by delving into the backgrounds of the principals (is the agency chairman a former subcommittee staffer?) or by determining whether the chairman's district receives an inordinate amount of benefits from the agency in question.

Oversight hearings, when they occur, need not be all-encompassing or involve billions of dollars to be important to investigators. In 1980, the *Washington Post* ran an article on an oversight investigation by the Senate Special Committee on Aging. The subject was a program intended to help the elderly poor refurbish run-down homes. Yet *Post* reporter Helen Dewar paid attention, even though, as she said, "in the billion-dollar-a-day business of official Washington, several thousand individual grants of up to $5000 apiece for new plumbing, floorboards, windows and the like hardly seems to merit a second glance." The compeling tales that resulted made Dewar's effort worthwhile. An investigator interested in a committee's oversight plans can read the committee's annual budget request. Also, the House Government Operations Committee publishes a report each year entitled "Oversight Plans of the Committees of the U.S. House of Representatives." The compilation is tentative, but nonetheless useful.

If an investigator wants to learn whether a congressional committee has held hearings or issued reports about a topic, one place to look is in the index published by Congressional Information Services Inc., a Washington-area business. A typical entry for a hearing will list the names and affiliations of all witnesses, when they testified and what they discussed.

Investigators who track hearings should be alert for further legislative action; that can be difficult. C. Fred Bergsten, an assistant secretary of the treasury under President Carter, noted in the *New York Times* that any program without permanent authorization from Congress must go through twenty-seven distinct steps before it is funded. The steps are repeated annually. After completing hearings, the subcommittee and full committee go through a mark-up, which means the language is revised line by line. Often drafts of the revised wording are available before the bill is adopted. If even one word is changed from the bill as introduced, an investigator might ask why, and at whose behest. In the legislative arena, substitution of an "and" for an "or" can alter a bill significantly. If a formula for distributing funds is at stake, the shift of just one decimal point can mean the gain or loss of millions of dollars for a state.

When a majority of subcommittee and committee members agree to the revised language, the bill is reported to the full chamber. An actual report is prepared; it can be a valuable document. The report contains dissenting views, if any. It also generally contains a section-by-section analysis of the bill, ways in which the bill would change existing laws, what the Congressional Budget Office thinks it will cost taxpayers over five years and interesting (maybe scathing) exchanges of correspondence between committee members and bureaucrats regarding the proposed legislation.

After a bill is reported from a House committee, it almost always goes to the House Rules Committee where ground rules for floor debate are determined. The bill, with its "rule," is then put on a schedule for floor debate. (In the Senate, there is no rules committee.) If the chamber approves the bill as reported by committee or as amended on the floor, it must be

approved by the other chamber in identical form in order to go
to the president.

When there are differences between the House and
Senate versions, a conference committee is named. These committees are different from regular committees, and each has its
own characteristics. Conference committees are not permanent entities; they go out of existence after resolving the differences over a particular bill. Each conference committee has
informal procedures by which it operates, and each issues a
report explaining what it has done. During a conference, an
investigator can often obtain a comparison sheet showing current law, what the House bill would do and what the Senate bill
would do. This sheet makes a handy scorecard during conference committee debate. Comparison sheets are sometimes
available at the House or Senate committee that originally
handled the legislation.

Appointment of conferees can be of interest to an
investigator in that nearly one-fourth of all bills enacted into
law—including almost every appropriations measure—are
products of conference committee activity. In the Senate, the
common practice is for the presiding officer to appoint the conferees after talking to the chairman of the committee that has
jurisdiction over the legislation. In the House, it is the speaker
who appoints the conferees; he, too, generally talks first to the
appropriate committee chairman. The speaker is supposed to
appoint authors of principal amendments to the legislation
when those amendments will be negotiating points. Despite the
rules, there is room for discretion in the selection of conferees.
Chairmen have been accused of stacking the conferees in favor
of their own personal beliefs rather than in favor of the
majority's will. There have also been charges that senior
members are named too frequently, even though their beliefs
might be out of step with the majority.

Conference committees and all other committees usually
meet in open session, a change from the early 1970s and before.
Closed meetings still occur, however. In order to have them,
some committees use the excuse that meeting rooms are too

small to allow for public attendance. "After being painstaking-
ly pried open to the public and press under rules adopted by
both houses in 1973 and 1975, doors are once again slamming
shut across Capitol Hill," noted reporter Peter Stuart of the
Christian Science Monitor in 1981.

Recently, several appropriations subcommittees have
closed their mark-ups of money bills. Said one House subcommittee staffer, "The members feel closed sessions facilitate
their discussion of the issues and the amounts to be ap-
propriated. When the mark-ups were open, the members felt it
was a madhouse, with people rushing in and out and trying to
command their attention. Now, the staff simply announces the
results at the end of the mark-up." There are other ways
around open meetings besides closing the doors to the public.
Reid of the *Washington Post* described one subcommittee mark-
up in which the two participating senators and their staffs
thumbed their noses at openness by huddling with their backs
to the audience and talking inaudibly. After matters were
settled, only then did the senators face the audience. At that
time, one of them made a motion incorporating their ageements
into the legislation, and the "open" mark-up ended.

No matter what the committee or how it operates, an
investigator cannot go wrong by focusing on the chairman.
Even though chairmen lack the absolute authority they once
held on the basis of seniority alone, there is plenty of authority
remaining. (That is true, though to a lesser extent, of the ranking minority party member on each committee and subcommittee.) When Republican Senator Strom Thurmond of South
Carolina took over the Judiciary Committee in 1981, he abolish-
ed one of its subcommittees, created a new, controversial one,
appointed the chairmen of each of the nine subcommittees and
slashed the committee's budget by $1.25 million.

Because there are so many committees and subcommittees, the majority party has multiple power bases. During 1980,
slightly more than half of all House Democrats chaired a committee or subcommittee. In the Senate, almost 90 percent of the
Democrats held one or more chairmanships. These chairmen

control dozens of professional staff members who serve at their pleasure. The staffers often think of themselves as employees of the chairman (or ranking minority member) rather than of the committee.

Control of a committee staff means having the ability to conduct investigations, or to block someone else from having the manpower to conduct one. When a chairman introduces legislation related to his committee's jurisdiction, it is almost certain the bill will get a hearing if he wants it to. A chairman can singlehandedly control the fate of entire regions. Writing in 1980 about Representative Phillip Burton, a California Democrat, *Washington Post* reporter Ward Sinclair said Burton's chairmanship of the national parks and insular affairs subcommittee made him ruler of an empire on which the sun never set. (The empire encompassed Guam, American Samoa and the Northern Marianas in the far Pacific as well as the Virgin Islands and Puerto Rico in the Atlantic.)

Though Sinclair chose Burton as the focus of his article, he could have picked other chairmen. "In truth, this [Burton's influence] isn't at all odd on Capitol Hill, " Sinclair said. "Dozens of relatively obscure subcommittees, dealing with often obscure issues, are the seats of little sub-governments and sources of imposing power."

Almost every chairman has his share of "pork barrel" projects to dole out, projects benefitting only one locale, often at substantial public expense. One House committee and its Senate counterpart, for example, have a stranglehold on the construction of federal office buildings. Suggestions for building sites based on careful study by the executive branch reportedly have been ignored by the committee chairmen, who instead push building construction in their own districts or the districts of favored colleagues.

An investigator can get advance notice of what a chairman plans to do in a committee by studying the proposed committee budget when it is presented to the full chamber for approval. The budget is reported as a bill and a committee report with its wealth of information is issued. Budget requests are published in the *Congressional Record*, too. In early 1981 an investigator could have learned that the Senate Committee on Governmental Affairs wanted $4.7 million for staff and other expenses in order to conduct inquiries. Donald Baker of the *Washington Post* reported in 1981 that Senator Charles Mathias, a Maryland Republican, had acquired new-found power because of his chairmanship of the Rules and Administration Committee; the committee approved budget requests from other panels. The chairmen of those other panels, often with more power and prestige than Mathias, nonetheless came before him as "suppliants," Baker said.

If a committee asks for additional money during the year, that might signify something important. A mid-year request for an extra $200,000 by the Senate Judiciary Committee tipped off reporters to that committee's investigation into the Libyan dealings of President Carter's brother Billy.

How a committee spends its money can be determined by scrutinizing the reports of the House clerk and Senate secretary. Seemingly insignificant expenditures can be wasteful, as when a House committee issued a history of its first twenty years at a cost of over $325,000. Part of that amount was paid to a former committee member hired as a $47,500 per year consultant.

When an investigator understands the relationship between a committee's Democrats and Republicans, he can more easily follow the committee's work. Some committees are relatively non-partisan and harmonious, while others are ineffective in legislating and oversight because of partisan bitterness. (At times intra-party divisions cause problems, too.) There was trouble in 1980-81 when House Republicans complained of being shortchanged on committee seats. *Washington Star* reporters Mary Thornton and Roberta Hornig noted that Senate Majority Leader Howard Baker was supporting House Republicans by threatening to stack Senate panels against the Democrats. "Baker's statement was in direct contrast to his optimistic cooperation pledge after formally meeting with [House Speaker Tip] O'Neill earlier this week," the *Star* reporters said.

Minority party members usually have some say in hiring aides, though here, too, staffing is not always proportional. An investigator should cultivate minority party committee members and their staffers. Susan Hammond and Harrison Fox note in their book *Congressional Staffs* that minority professionals develop policy alternatives to what is being proposed by the majority and gather information independently. When majority party committee staffers are secretive, minority staffers may be garrulous.

Many students of Congress believe committee staffers wield more influence than members of Congress themselves; some are unparalleled experts. In 1981 the *Washington Post* profiled staff directors of the fifteen Senate committees, all newly controlled by Republicans. The story stressed the staff directors' diverse backgrounds, their youth (almost all were under forty) and the power they would possess. "They are the behind-the-scenes movers and shakers in the new Republican-controlled Senate," wrote reporters Helen Dewar and Ward Sinclair. It is unarguable that some committee staff professional exercise great authority, if for no other reason than the source of the authority—the member of Congress—has so little time.

An investigator who regularly follows a committee should cultivate not only its professional and clerical staffers, but also personal congressional staffers who work closely with the committee. A congressman without the power to hire staffers for a committee important to him may entrust committee chores to a loyal personal aide. Another tip for an investigator tracking a committee is to study the committee's rules. Even though a chairman can be arbitrary, committee rules sometimes reduce that arbitrariness. An investigator who can recognize an end-run around the rules is in a better position than one who cannot. Every panel publishes its rules somewhere—in a pamphlet, in its legislative calendar, in the *Congressional Record* or in a booklet compiling all House or Senate committee rules.

Following the Dollar Through Congress

Until the mid-1970s, Congress handled the budget in a haphazard manner. That has changed. Congress now has a timetable for authorizing and appropriating money for each item funded by the federal government. The process sometimes breaks down, but a knowledgeable investigator can find the information he needs. (The model budget process is described in many sources, including the official budget booklet sent by the president to Congress every January.)

An investigator who wants to follow the battles over a particular program from beginning to end should begin long before the president's budget is submitted to the House and Senate. A great deal of tugging among the private interests, federal agencies, White House Office of Management and Budget and the president himself goes on in private. Formulation of the fiscal 1982 budget (for the year starting October 1, 1981) actually began in early 1980. But few investigators paid attention to the 1982 figures until they were released by the White House in early 1981.

Once the president's proposals are turned over to Congress, there are endless possibilities for the investigator. Congress can approve, modify or disapprove the proposals. It can change funding levels, eliminate items or add programs not requested by the president. On the income side, Congress can endorse legislation which sets tax levels or, in other ways, increases or decreases receipts.

The *Washington Post*, besides following the budget debate in numerous authorizing and appropriating committees of Congress, has published articles relating the multi-billion-dollar figures to individual people, groups or locales. Ward Sinclair traced the way in which a cutback in one obscure part of the budget played havoc with the library at Durham Technical Institute, a two-year college in North Carolina. T.R. Reid described how approximately half a billion dollars would be channeled to Fort Wayne, Indiana—about $2500 for each resident. Nicholas Lemann looked at the dilemma of a fiscally conservative congressman who "built a career around opposition to the federal deficit," but who hated to see his district hurt by cutbacks. Spencer Rich reported how 25 percent of the budget would aid senior citizens.

Investigators who prefer to focus on the larger view can find plenty to look at. They can dig into "uncontrollable spending," the programs like Social Security and Medicare which Congress has decided Americans are entitled to year after year, without question. These programs account for more than 75 cents of every dollar; when Congress debates a $700 billion annual budget, it is actually deciding how to allocate only one-fourth of that amount, at most.

Robert Samuelson of the *National Journal* focused on loan guarantees, federal obligations that fail to show up in budget deficit totals and which make the deficit seem much smaller—and thus more politically acceptable—than it truly is. Describing such fraud, Samuelson cited $140 million intended to help fishermen buy new boats, and $1 billion to encourage businesses to relocate in rural America. These amounts were nowhere to be seen in the budget, despite its customary mind-numbing detail. "Yet these programs. . .are as real as the Washington Monument," Samuelson said. "They certify the ingenuity of politicians and bureaucrats, who crave the best of both worlds—extra plums for constituents without the extra pain of higher taxes." Speaking of the same fraud, Eileen Shanahan of the *Washington Star* said "it is probably too much to hope that either President Reagan or the Congress will vote for full truth in government lending by putting all these loans and loan guarantees back into the budget." James O'Shea of the *Chicago Tribune* investigated one little-known entity through which off-budget funding was accomplished, the Federal Financing Bank.

Tracking Legislation Through the House and Senate

Even though most bills never emerge from committee, some—including most appropriations bills emerging from budget debate—do clear the hurdles. If that happens, they are placed on a House calendar for floor debate. Or they go to the

Senate floor after that body's leadership is convinced a time agreement has been reached to eventually end debate. An investigator will understand what happens to a bill on the floor only by studying the often arcane rules of each chamber. Senate and House floor procedures are very different—learning about just one does not suffice. Thorough summaries are contained in booklets written by congressional employees. The booklets are often available free, or can be bought from the Government Printing Office. *Enactment of a Law: Procedural Steps in the Legislative Process* and *Senate Legislative Procedural Flow (and Related House Action)* are two examples.

To cover Senate floor debate well, a reporter must be there in person, in the portion of the galleries reserved for the media. (Other investigators can sit in the public galleries, though note-taking is forbidden there.) House floor debate can be covered in person or by television; proceedings are shown on cable television systems across the United States. Offices on Capitol Hill receive House floor debate on their sets through a closed-circuit system. Impending votes are signalled through a system of lights and buzzers attached to clocks in congressional office buildings. (The system is explained on directories scattered throughout the buildings.) An investigator can also keep informed of happenings on the House or Senate floor by calling the press galleries, by dialing the Democratic or Republican cloakrooms or by talking to staffers in the offices of House and Senate leaders, especially the speaker of the House and the Senate majority leader. Whenever, feasible, an advance schedule is published in the *Congressional Record*.

To be well prepared, an investigator should be familiar with the bill that is the subject of debate. A copy of the bill as first introduced can be obtained from the sponsor, from the House Document Room (on the second floor of the Capitol) or from the Senate Document Room (on the third floor). The investigator should also have the bill as revised in whatever committees it was referred to; the accompanying report issued by the committee, which will contain dissents; the House whip advisory, usually a one-page summary of the bill prepared by the party leadership; and summaries by other political party organizations in Congress such as the House Democratic Study Group and the House Republican Conference. These summaries are found more readily in the House than in the Senate. As the most important bills wind through committees, they are tracked by *Congressional Quarterly Weekly Report;* background articles in that magazine are usually accurate.

An investigator trying to keep track of numerous bills simultaneously will find the *Digest of Public General Bills and Resolutions* useful. It is compiled by the Congressional Research Service in the Library of Congress and is available for purchase through the Government Printing Office, or free for consulting at the Library of Congress or other reference libraries. Each year there are cumulative editions, frequent supplements, and a year-end edition. The computerized version is updated repeatedly. One part includes a summary of every bill that has become law during the current Congress, along with dates of House and Senate actions that led to passage. Another part lists House and Senate bills that are not law, but on which some action has been taken. The actual digest of every bill comes next, in numerical order. If a measure is identical to one introduced earlier in the same session, that is noted. Following the digest of all bills is a listing of each member of Congress and the legislation he has sponsored or co-sponsored. There is also an index of bills by subject.

The House and Senate calendars—available in the document rooms—are not as comprehensive, but are more current. The House version, officially titled "Calendars of the United States House of Representatives and History of Legislation," is published daily when the House is in session. Each issue is cumulative. Every Monday there is a subject index of all House and Senate legislation which has been reported by committees and acted upon by either chamber. In a normal House calendar, the first section lists bills in House-Senate conferences, by date. The names of all representatives and senators participating in the conference are given, and issuance of the conference report is noted by number and date. The same day's calendar lists bills that have made it through conference, noting when they became law and the number of the law. Listed next are all items (bills through committee, presidential messages and other matters) referred to various calendars—the Union Calendar, the House Calendar, the calendar for private bills, the consent calendar for allegedly non-controversial bills and the calendar of motions for discharging a bill from committee consideration.

The Union Calendar is the most heavily scheduled—on it go most bills involving money. The House Calendar is less cluttered, because it is for bills unrelated to money; thus, a report from the Committee on Standards of Official Conduct concerning censure of a member of the House would be on this calendar. A bill to compensate the victim of Army drug experiments would probably be placed on the Private Calendar, reserved for measures involving one person. The Consent Calendar consists of bills—usually non-controversial—that have been taken from the House or Union calendars; they must receive two-thirds approval. The Discharge Calendar is used infrequently, by a member who believes that a committee to which a bill has been referred has no intention of discussing that bill. A motion for discharge cannot be filed until a committee has held a bill at least thirty days. The last section of the daily House publication lists, in numerical order, all House and Senate bills that have passed either or both chambers, as well as bills pending on the calendars.

The Senate publication, officially called the "Calendar of Business," is not so useful as the House version. It is issued daily when the Senate is working. Its main limitations are that it is not cumulative, nor is it indexed.

The Support Staffs of Congress

Congress has hundreds of employees who are neither part of any member's personal staff nor on any committee or sub-committee. These "internal staffers" have deceptively innocuous titles such as "doorkeeper," "clerk of the House," or "secretary of the Senate." There are also support staffs in the

General Accounting Office, Congressional Research Service, Office of Technology Assessment and Congressional Budget Office who supply invaluable information.

First, the internal staffers. In the Senate, for example, the office of the secretary and the office of the sergeant at arms do much of the administrative work. In 1980 their combined staffs topped 1300 people. *Congressional Quarterly Weekly Report* noted that facilities and services provided included a cabinet shop, the Senate pages, printing and duplicating, a recording studio, a barber shop and post office. During 1980, then Senate Majority Leader Robert Byrd inserted lectures about the internal offices into the *Congressional Record*. The lectures contain much information of potential use to investigators.

The General Accounting Office is the most visible of the support arms; its reports are circulated widely among journalists. In a "60 Minutes" profile of GAO, Dan Rather said "hardly a day passes without a news story based on the findings of a GAO investigation." Veteran Washington correspondent Clark Mollenhoff stresses the usefulness of GAO reports. In his book *Investigative Reporting* he provides examples of how he used the reports both as tools to launch investigations and as authoritative background on subjects he was studying. George Anthan, a *Des Moines Register* Washington correspondent, said, "I've done a lot of stories, major stories, that have received signficant play, from GAO reports." With a staff topping 5000, the agency produces about 1000 reports annually—an average of about four every working day. It is almost a cliche to call GAO "the watchdog arm of Congress."

Often a GAO report is a self-contained story, though what many investigators fail to track is the lack of follow-up on GAO's recommendations. A 1980 Common Cause study noted how consistently GAO suggestions are ignored after initial publicity. GAO makes it easy for investigators to trace this phenomenon by publishing an annual compilation for the House and Senate Appropriations committees detailing recommendations "on which satisfactory legislative or administrative actions have not been taken." Morton Mintz of the *Washington Post* reported in 1981 that GAO told the Defense Department how it could save at least $4 billion annually. The recommendations were culled from "repeated audits" by "1000 GAO accountants and other professionals continuously studying Pentagon programs." Although most GAO reports are initiated in-house, about one third are written at the request of a congressional committee and some are asked for by individual members of Congress. Numerous reports are required by law—in a recent year, Congress passed eleven bills with requirements for GAO audits. In addition, a 1970 law ordered GAO to perform cost-benefit analyses of federal programs.

The Congressional Research Service, part of the Library of Congress, had about 850 employees in 1981. CRS is prohibited from releasing its work to the public unless authorized by the member of Congress or congressional committee requesting the information. In 1980, CRS received about 330,000 congressional queries. Occasionally a book-length report emerges from CRS that catches the attention of journalists and other investigators. The *New York Times* in 1980 told of a 600-page CRS publication called *U.S.-Soviet Military Balance, Concepts and Capabilities, 1960-1980.* It was written by the service's senior specialist on national defense. The *Times* noted that the book was being read at the Central Intelligence Agency, Pentagon and Soviet and Chinese embassies.

CRS "Issue Briefs" can be of great help to an investigator, though they are difficult to obtain. One way is to request specific titles through a congressional office. Available are about 300 briefs, updated regularly. New briefs are published and older ones dropped from the current file as the topics before Congress change. A list of current briefs can be found in the monthly *Update,* which also contains summaries of new CRS reports. The *CRS Review,* another monthly, provides highlights from CRS analyses of topics that are the talk of Congress, such as gasohol or the causes of inflation.

By law, CRS provides information to congressional committees. For example, at the start of each Congress, CRS gives each committee a list of programs under its jurisdiction that are ready to expire, along with another list of topics that the committee might want to analyze in depth. Like GAO, the service had specialists in almost every area. The specialties within CRS are mandated by Congress, and include education, housing, labor and employment, money and banking, veterans' affairs and others.

Although CRS is supposed to be used seriously and on a non-partisan basis, there are abuses. Some members, for instance, have been caught asking CRS to produce research papers for high school students, to trace their family genealogy, or to write speeches for a congressman to give before private groups.

The Office of Technology Assessment is the smallest of the four adjuncts; it had approximately 130 employees in 1981. Congress established the office to help evaluate the effects of scientific advances on government policy. An example of the office's work was assessing proposals for oil exploration and leasing on the Outer Continental Shelf. Most of the studies by OTA are undertaken at the request of congressional committees; the reports are available to investigators.

The office is perhaps closer to nitty-gritty politics than it would like—policy is set by a board consisting of three Democratic and three Republican senators plus three Democratic and three Republican House members. Senator Ted Stevens, an Alaska Republican, chaired the board in 1981; the chairmanship rotates every two years. The board hires OTA's director.

The Congressional Budget Office is the legislative branch counterpart to the White House Office of Management and Budget. Created in 1974 as part of Congress' new budget process, the office had about 200 employees in 1981. The professional staffers were divided into these units: budget analysis, fiscal analysis, tax analysis, human resources and community development, natural resources and commerce, national security and international affairs. For following money bills through Congress, CBO "scorecards" are useful. The office delves into "sexier" topics, too, issuing publicly available reports on such matters as the costs and benefits of decontrolling oil prices, long-run costs of the M-X missile and rising hospital charges. CBO cost estimates may differ from White House estimates.

CBO's director is appointed by Congress and can be removed by resolution of either chamber, so the director tries to be non-partisan. The office's first responsibility is to help the House and Senate Budget committees. The next priority is to aid the Appropriations committees, the House Ways and Means Committee and the Senate Finance Committee. Other committees may also request studies through the chairman or ranking minority member.

Members of Congress use the four support arms partly to keep up with the expertise in the executive branch. The pinnacle of the executive branch—the White House—will be examined in the next chapter.

The White House

P robably no segment of the Washington media corps is considered so prestigious as the White House correspondents. Yet those same correspondents are perhaps the most criticized by outside journalistic obervers. Not all the insiders are impressed, either. Lou Cannon, now covering the Reagan White House for the *Washington Post*, commented a few years ago that a shortcoming of White House coverage is "hyperactivity, which allows scant time for thought or evaluation. The institution of the Presidency, as practiced in the jet age, envelops everyone in motion for the sake of motion, in reams of paper, in too much waiting. . .It is missing the mark to call this 'handout journalism.' It is worse than that. It is mindless journalism." In 1981, Cannon said he had modified his views. "The major newspapers and the networks are using teams to cover the White House in most cases, and a more reflective approach has taken hold." As an example, Cannon said his partner Lee

Lescaze was at the White House that day covering the breaking news, while Cannon was conducting interviews for a Sunday article on why the administration had been so slow to fill agency jobs.

Hugh Sidey, syndicated columnist and *Time* correspondent, railed in 1981 that the Presidency was being "interfered with by the media—from television to newsletters—which has grown too big for its assigned quarters and too dedicated to drama and entertainment to claim the White House vantage point on its old credentials of informing and enlightening the people." Sidey, calling the media a "huge special interest," suggested that White House reporters be removed from the West Wing.

In short, almost everyone agrees there is room for improvement in coverage of the White House.

Accredited Journalists, Non-Accredited Investigators and the Press Office

About 1300 journalists had White House credentials in early 1981, plus several hundred broadcast technicians. Congressional accreditation is necessary for a permanent White House pass. Decisions about whom to accredit are made by the White House press office. Investigators without official credentials can get into the White House complex by being placed on an access list, intended for those with no need for a permanent credential, but who may go to the White House once a month or so. A Secret Service check is performed after an investigator asks to be put on the access list so that when he calls the press office in advance for permission to enter the grounds, his name can be located on a computer printout by the security guards. Investigators without a permanent pass or a spot on the access list must set up interviews with White House staffers and be cleared through the gate on a one-time basis. If possible, an investigator should call a day in advance for clearance. He will have to provide his full name, birthdate, Social Security number and media affiliation.

When the president leaves the White House complex to travel inside Washington, only journalists with permanent credentials from the White House, a congressional gallery, the State Department, Secret Service or metropolitan police can be inside the roped-off area wherever the president is speaking. When the president travels outside Washington, persons wanting to accompany him must obtain trip passes through the White House transportation office; it handles plane or bus arrangements and lodging. On some trips, all those wanting to go can be accommodated. On other trips, not all requests can be granted. One observer commented, "The demand for seats was much greater when President Reagan took his first trip to California than it was when President Carter would return to Plains, Georgia."

During the Carter administration, investigators who were not White House regulars often found it easier to obtain information from the part of the press operation called the Office of Media Liaison. While the main press office is located in the West Wing of the White House, the media liaison staff is found next to the White House in the Old Executive Office Building. The media liaison staff exists, however, mainly to help out-of-town journalists. (In 1981, the Reagan administration hired a press aide away from a Republican senator to direct the Office of Media Liaison.)

Most Washington-based correspondents, therefore, must call the press office itself. Press secretary James Brady, before he was seriously wounded by a would-be presidential assassin, was unlikely to be the person returning the call; the *Post's* Lescaze reported in early 1981 that Brady was "a difficult man to track down." Callers were more likely to talk with one of the two deputy press secretaries, either of the two assistant press secretaries, an aide designated to handle questions from the foreign media, or other staffers.

"We use the press office every day for all kinds of routine things," Cannon said. "Schedules, briefings, planning purposes, an official White House response to an announcement from elsewhere, you name it. I also try to establish a good relationship to get background, unofficial guidance that might steer me away from non-story stories."

Cannon does not shy away from using press office staffers as sources. "If one of them has been inside a meeting, his account can be just as reliable as the account of a Cabinet officer. . .You have to take it on a case-by-case basis."

Accredited correspondents who work within the White House press office will find staffers just a few yards away. News releases and other official documents are easily available. Announcements are made by press office staffers over a loudspeaker system. The president's daily schedule is posted. It is also printed in the *Washington Post* and *Washington Star* and put on a telephone recording.

"I spend eight to twelve hours a day in the press area," said Robert Pierpoint of CBS-TV during a 1980 interview, shortly before he switched to the State Department. "I've only been on Capitol Hill once in the last year." Many White House correspondents complain about how confining the beat is, how difficult it can be to reach anybody except the press office staff. A correspondent for a major newspaper chain told John Hyde of the *Des Moines Register* Washington Bureau: "It's like covering General Motors...you wait in the anteroom until the secretary comes out and tells you what decision has been made. What you miss is anything about why the decision was made, or who made it, or for what reason." Hyde, in his article on the Reagan press office, quoted another White House regular frustrated at being unable to reach Martin Anderson, Reagan's top domestic policy advisor. The reporter said he sent Anderson a telegram reading, "If you are being held against your will, raise and lower your windowshade three times."

Reporters covering the White House have formed a White House Correspondents Association, a group which occasionally discusses problems of coverage with the press secretary. Unlike the ruling organizations in the congressional galleries, the White House group has no say over who is accredited. In truth, the association is largely a social club, whose main activity is an annual dinner. Membership in the association is open to non-regulars; the main requirement is payment of a small annual fee. In early 1981 there were about 600 dues payers. Pierpoint of CBS was president; the other officers and board members were from NBC News, RKO General Broadcasting, *Newsweek, New Republic, the Washington Post, Washington Star, Los Angeles Times* and *New Orleans Times-Picayune.*

The press secretary is so firmly in control that he becomes a focal point of the media. Not only does he explain the news: sometimes he is the news. This accounts for lengthy profiles of Brady in early 1981. Three days after Elisabeth Bumiller's *Washington Post* profile of Brady appeared, Jacqueline Trescott of the *Post* did a profile of Karna Small, who had just been named deputy press secretary to President Reagan.

When interviewing press aides, or other White House staffers, investigators need to understand the language of attribution. This is a problem throughout Washington, but appears to be especially serious at the White House, the State Department and the Pentagon. In administration after administration, information has been conveyed with conditions attached. Not even experienced reporters agree on the precise meaning of the terms, though one version of the rules goes like this: "Not-for-attribution" means it is all right to use the information and to specify the approximate position of the source, but the name of the source must be withheld. "On background" means it is all right to attribute the information to a vague source such as "high officials." "Off-the-record" means that the entire interview or briefing has been a non-happening. Cannon says many sources say information is off-the-record when they mean not-for-attribution.

Covering News from the White House

The daily briefing by the press secretary or one of his deputies is attended by numerous investigators. (Television cameras and still photographs are banned, however.) The briefings, usually held at mid-day, are designed to convey official presidential positions. Cannon does not see this practice as all bad: "If it doesn't do anything else for you, it will tell you what the White House wants to say that day." The problem is that the briefer can make routine announcements and be assured of favorable coverage. In his book *Reporting: An Inside View*, Cannon says "the briefings, scorned though they may be, provide the vast bulk of the White House news." Cannon tries to use the briefings as "the starting point for a story, not the whole story."

Walter Wurfel, a Washington vice-president for Gannett Co. who worked in the Carter White House press office, says "Often the briefings are a waste of time. Your chances of getting called on if you're not a regular are slim if it's a hot news day. You can always walk up to the briefer afterwards and ask your question, though. Sometimes you'll find Cabinet secretaries and other officials at the briefing, though the questions to them tend to be tightly controlled." Transcripts of the briefings are available at the press office for investigators who cannot attend.

Another type of pack coverage is the news conference, held in the Old Executive Office Building; no ban on filming the remarks is imposed. President Reagan said in early 1981 that he would hold at least one nationally televised session a month, plus have smaller, informal sessions with selected reporters. Many investigators find the televised conferences a waste of time—the chance of being called upon is slim, coverage can be accomplished just as well in front of the TV set, and anyone working on an exclusive story would not want to tip off competitors by asking a question in front of them.

Presidential news conferences were in the news in early 1981. Brady announced several changes in the format, following suggestions from a blue-ribbon panel that included past White House correspondents and press secretaries. The changes were designed to make the televised conferences more orderly. The first smaller, informal non-televised meeting between Reagan and the media gave five newspaper reporters a chance to question the president. Each of the papers ran stories after the event. *Washington Post* political columnist David Broder praised the changes, saying "we in the press have a professional obligation to try to make this experiment work. It is clearly in the public interest to facilitate regular exchanges at close range between the president and the reporters who cover him most frequently." Broder added he would do his part by staying away from the televised events, as he had for five years.

Broder believes many ways exist to cover the White House without spending hours at daily briefings and news conferences. Those ways will be the focus of the remainder of this chapter.

The White House Staff

So many investigators key on the president that sometimes it seems as if the White House is a one-person operation. Nothing could be farther from the truth. The president is surrounded by aides who can be first-rate sources of information. Generally, they are not as accessible as experts in Congress or in the agencies, but an investigator who cultivates White House sources will find that his efforts pay off.

Every president has top personal advisors. In the first year of the Reagan administration, three men fell into that category—Edwin Meese III, counselor to the president; James Baker III, chief of staff; and Michael Deaver, assistant to the president and deputy chief of staff. A *Wall Street Journal* page one feature referred to Meese as the "assistant president." A *Washington Post* feature on Baker ran four pages in a Sunday edition. Reporter Tony Kornheiser described the job this way: "Ideally, the chief of staff screens access to the president, gathers information, reduces it to digestible size, then presents it to the president without bias." What Baker told Kornheiser shows why an investigator would benefit from having top personal aides to the president as sources: "I know that most policy decisions are made in that Oval Office with two or three people sitting around, and I'm going to be one of those people. The fact of the matter is that it's going to be Mike Deaver, Ed Meese and myself."

Most White House staffers, even the top ones, try to maintain a low profile. But ways do exist for investigators to gather background on them. For up-to-date standard biographical information, an investigator can consult a newsletter published in early 1981 by Political Profiles Inc. The newsletter contains sketches of over eighty newly named White House staffers, including Meese, Baker and Deaver. On Inauguration Day 1981, the *Washington Star* and *Washington Post* each published profiles of important White House personnel. Another source is financial disclosure statements that must be filed annually by White House staffers at the level of GS-16 or above. In the Reagan White House, the financial disclosures are available to investigators in the office of the counsel to the president.

Numerous other White House staffers—the speechwriters, personnel officers, the counsel for legal affairs—fall into the same category as Meese, Baker and Deaver, though they are not so high in rank. In other words, these staffers are not policy experts, but they play a role in policy deliberations. Because they tend to be extremely loyal to the president, they may be less than candid with investigators—or they may be altogether inaccessible. That is no excuse, however, for investigators to stop trying to reach them.

The *Post's* Cannon says, "In most administrations there are a limited number of people who know what is going on and a far greater number of people who have a need to show that they know something. A reporter learns the real sources from the uninformed ones by painstaking trial and error." The trouble, Cannon adds, is that an investigator can become too dependent on the few good sources.

Nonetheless, stories appear regularly that are based, at least in part, on information from White House staffers. An investigator looking into the fate of a presidential proposal in Congress should talk to Max Friedersdorf, assistant to Reagan for legislative affairs. In early 1981, Friedersdorf had twelve professional employees under him whose jobs were to keep members of Congress informed and—when possible—happy. All had experience on Capitol Hill. Broder of the *Post* noted that

Friedersdorf's staff was trying to touch all bases, "being atten-
tive to the small but important gestures many members of Congress say they missed in the Carter years." These gestures included personal invitations to the White House welcome for the
former Iranian hostages, personal letters to each congressman
that listed the direct dial telephone numbers of Friedersdorf
and his staff and lunches with administrative assistants to
members of Congress. Hedrick Smith reported in the New York
Times that Reagan moved his State of the Union speech back a
day after learning that an important Democratic congressman
had a long-standing commitment outside Washington the night
the speech was originally scheduled.

When Steven Weisman of the New York Times
Washington Bureau wrote about Reagan's key appointments,
he interviewed E. Pendleton James, assistant to the president
for personnel. James' staff of fifty-four was doing its best to hire
only persons loyal to the president and his policies. James
talked freely about guidelines for hiring and firing. Weisman
noted that James had the responsibility of placing people in 750
Cabinet and sub-Cabinet positions, about 1000 upper-level jobs
just below sub-Cabinet rank and approximately 200 independent regulatory agency slots; he was also responsible for filling
perhaps fifty ambassadorships as well as vacancies on hundreds of advisory groups.

Unofficial personal advisors who fail to show up on flow
charts are important sources for investigators, if those advisors
can be persuaded to talk. In the Carter administration, perhaps
the most notable was Atlanta lawyer Charles Kirbo. Terence
Smith of the New York Times reported in 1980 that "little-
noticed by the press or public, Kirbo flies to Washington from
Atlanta every two weeks or so. He usually spends the day shuf-
fling through the corridors of the west wing of the White House,
dropping in. . .on key officials. . .After a day of low-key con-
sultations, Kirbo will get together with Mr. and Mrs. Carter,
usually over dinner and often afterwards, to discuss what he
has heard and to mull over any sensitive political problems that
may be on the president's mind. . .Although his role in the

White House is untitled, unsalaried, unnominated and unconfirmed, he clearly ranks at the top of the political pecking
order. He carries a White House pass and sleeps in the Lincoln
bedroom when he's in Washington."

In the Reagan administration, "kitchen cabinet" supporters identified early include Justin Dart, a wealthy
businessman; Holmes Tuttle, a car dealer and Republican Party
activist; and Earle Jorgensen, a steel company executive. All
three are rich, conservative Californians, over seventy years of
age, who are long-time social friends of the president. Cannon
said he sometimes succeeded in getting through to kitchen
cabinet members while working on a story.

Investigators covering the White House will find the same
quality of substantive expertise there that they find on Capitol
Hill or in the departments and agencies. The first place to look
for it is the White House Office of Management and Budget: its
personnel are located in the New and Old Executive Office
Buildings. The director of that office in 1981, David Stockman,
received a tremendous amount of coverage as he took the lead
in formulating President Reagan's $40 billion-plus package of
proposed budget cuts. The *Washington Post Magazine* put
Stockman's face on the cover, with the heading "Reagan's
Whiz Kid—the Stockman Saga: Thirteen Years Ago an Antiwar
Activist, Today Czar of a $700 Billion Budget." OMB's Office of
Budget Review has an overview that can help investigators.
"That's where I could get sources to straighten out numbers for
me," said Ed Dale, a former *New York Times* reporter named to
head OMB's public affairs office in 1981.

James Deakin, veteran Washington correspondent for the
St. Louis Post-Dispatch, said he covered OMB not only because
of its role in budget formulation, but also "because of its follow-
through. It keeps track of how agencies carry out legislation
and whether they do it within budget guidelines." With a
budget of about $30 million and a staff of around 600 (the
figures are from early 1981), OMB is small compared to almost
any regulatory agency or Cabinet department. Yet OMB has

substantial authority over the larger entities, making the office a lightning rod for dissatisfaction.

Congressional committees and OMB argue frequently over OMB-ordered cutbacks. When the House Foreign Affairs Committee expressed its opposition to closing thirteen American consulates around the world, the committee noted it was "deeply concerned" about cuts being "imposed on the Department of State" by OMB.

After the president makes known his overall budget priorities, it is OMB's job to tell each agency how large a slice of the pie that agency can expect. If an agency believes its portion is too small, the only way it can overturn OMB is to convince the President to ask for more from Congress.

Within OMB, there are experts on various topics. An example is Edward Sanders, who had responsibility for national security and international affairs under Presidents Nixon, Ford and Carter. Sanders, whose background includes a Ph.D. in economics from Yale University, left OMB in 1981 to become staff director of the Senate Foreign Relations Committee.

OMB divides the world into four chunks: national security and international affairs; economics and government; natural resources, energy and science; and human resources, veterans and labor. In 1981, a newly created assistant administrator was to ride herd on excessive government regulation and paperwork. OMB is one of the few White House subdivisions with a public affairs staff separate from the main press office.

The Office of Management and Budget is a main component of the Executive Office of the President (in contrast to the personal aides who constitute the White House Office). The units of the Executive Office tend to employ persons who are experts in specific topics. In the Carter administration, perhaps the most influential unit besides OMB was the Domestic Policy Staff, renamed the Office of Policy Development under Reagan. In 1980, it had fifty-four employees, thirty of whom were professionals. Despite its small size, it had vast influence over the content of legislation. As *Congressional Quarterly Weekly*

Report noted, "All policy questions—except for defense and foreign policy issues—are cleared with DPS. . .It oversees the framing of bills in the executive agencies. It resolves conflicting agency proposals. Often, it has the last word on the shape of an administration bill before it is sent to Capitol Hill." DPS worked closely with OMB as a clearinghouse. Stuart Eizenstat, President Carter's DPS chief, referred to the "DPS-OMB process." OMB was consulted to determine whether legislative priorities meshed with budget realities.

Sometimes DPS tried to prevent the administration from appearing divided. The *Washington Star* reported in late 1980 that an associate director of the Domestic Policy Staff told lawyers in the Justice Department to stay away from a politically sensitive proceeding at the International Trade Commission regarding foreign auto import quotas. The Justice Department planned to oppose import quotas; the Department of Transportation took a position more protective of domestic automakers.

In the Reagan administration, Martin Anderson, an economist, was named to the spot Eizenstat had held under Carter. Anderson had worked in the Nixon White House, leaving to join a conservative think tank called the Hoover Institution, before becoming Reagan's issues advisor during the 1976 and 1980 presidential campaigns.

Other units of the Executive Office were sometimes valuable places for investigators to go for information under Carter; they were expected to be of value under Reagan, too. Speaking of these units, the *Post-Dispatch's* Deakin wondered "How many reporters know that you'll find a government within a government in the White House?"

The National Security Council employs geographical experts, just as the State Department does. In 1981 it had about eighty employees. During the Carter years, it was headed by Zbigniew Brzezinski, assistant for national security affairs. Battles between Brzezinski and the secretary of state made headlines regularly. The battles happened so often, in fact, that President Reagan made it clear there would be no celebrities like Brzezinski in his Executive Office. Reagan said Richard

Allen, his national security advisor, would keep a low profile and not act as a rival to the secretary of state.

Other units of the Executive Office that can be useful to investigators include the Council of Economic Advisors (thirty-eight employees in 1980), the Office of the U.S. Trade Representative (forty-two employees) and the Office of Science and Technology Policy (thirty-three employees). There is nothing sacred about the organizational chart, however. In early 1981 Reagan announced he was abolishing the ninety-employee Council on Wage and Price Stability.

White House staffers have support personnel who are potential sources. For instance, William Gulley, head of the White House Military Affairs Office for eleven years, said in his 1980 book, *Breaking Cover,* that he dispensed money from a secret multi-million dollar fund, money sometimes spent illegally at the order of the president. The *Wall Street Journal* in 1980 ran an interesting, if not earth-shaking, story on the White House budget—over $3 million was allotted for buildings and grounds. The executive chef was paid $42,000. A maid received $11,000. The 1980 electric bill was estimated at $190,000. The White House budget is published annually as part of the president's overall budget documentation. When the Reagan administration decided to fire about one-third of the operations staff, Maureen Santini of the Associated Press reported that the new president was breaking precedent by dismissing "the non-political workers who normally remain even when the president leaves. They fill technical and non-political jobs such as accountants, secretaries, mail openers and building manager."

The first lady and the vice president have their own staffs that can be of use to investigators. The first lady—at least since Eleanor Roosevelt—has always chosen a project to promote. Rosalynn Carter directed an inquiry into the United States' mental health care system. Nancy Reagan in early 1981 singled out the Foster Grandparents program as her special interest.

Joy Billington noted in the *Washington Star* that the first lady often makes news, as opposed to times past: "Today schedules are posted, a recording announces daily activities, and first ladies frequently jet around the nation nurturing their projects. . .And they are not paid for it." Taxpayer money is involved, though. The first lady's staff is paid well. When Mabel Brandon was named White House social secretary in early 1981, the *Washington Post* reported she would be paid between $45,000 and $50,000.

The way Gretchen Poston, social secretary in the Carter White House, handled her job was an interesting story for investigators who view the president and first lady as arbiters of the nation's cultural heritage. The Carters were often thought of as backwoods hicks by high society, but Poston brought Vladimir Horowitz and Mstislav Rostropovich to entertain at the White House, as well as Willie Nelson and Dolly Parton.

When Mrs. Reagan chose Sheila Patton as her press secretary in 1981 (at about $38,000 a year), the *Washington Post* and *Washington Star* both profiled Patton. An investigator should cultivate the press secretary in anticipation of those times when there is important information to be gained. For example, an investigator interested in South America could have interviewed Mrs. Carter after she headed the U.S. delegation at the inauguration of Peru's new president.

The vice president has a staff that will sometimes help an investigator, and may even provide information contradicting the White House line if there is ill feeling between the president and vice president. Less than a month after taking office Vice President George Bush named fifty-six personal staffers, including his own press secretary, his own congressional liaison, his own aide for national security and his own assistant for domestic policy. Sometimes the vice president takes the lead on an issue as when Bush announced the formation of a federal task force to aid the city of Atlanta in its investigation of black children being murdered. Bush and one of his staffers also had primary responsibility for directing the Presidential Task Force on Regulatory Relief. Most of Bush's staff is located near his work space in the Old Executive Office Building. Other staffers work from the vice president's West Wing office or from his office on Capitol Hill.

A White House staffer not mentioned until now is one whose main job is to help the president and vice president as party politicians, rather than as government policy makers. Franklin Nofziger, assistant to the president for political affairs, was tapped by President Reagan to coordinate party objectives with the Republican National Committee. Broder of the *Washington Post* devoted an article to Richard Williamson, assigned to sell Reagan's budget cuts to the nation's governors and mayors.

Washington Star political columnists Jack Germond and Jules Witcover, noting the Republicans were still weak in the South, reported that Lee Atwater, a South Carolina politico, "is in line for a place on the Reagan political staff with specific responsibility for liaison with Republican organizations in the South." Germond and Witcover said Atwater would be doing the same thing that Harry Dent, also from South Carolina, did in the Nixon White House. When Reagan tapped Elizabeth Dole as his assistant for public liaison, the *Star's* White House correspondent Jeremiah O'Leary reported that the post "is a politically oriented one in which the occupant is expected to drum up support for the president's programs and policies across a broad spectrum of special interests, such as women, senior citizens, ethnic groups and occupational interests." Anne Wexler, who held the job in the Carter administration, was sometimes a good source for investigators looking into politics at the White House.

When incumbent Carter was running for re-election in 1980, he did not hesitate to use political aides paid with public dollars to his own advantage. Francis Clines of the *New York Times* reported in 1980 that Carter had invited as many as 400 local politicians and other leaders from each of the states to the White House. Cabinet officers and other administration officials had fanned out across the country as surrogates for Carter. The Federal Election Commission ruled that if any portion of a Carter aide's trip were political, the entire trip had to be paid for by Carter's re-election committee, not with travel funds from the United States treasury.

Documents Useful for Investigating the White House

Just as with Congress, the agencies, the courts and the private interests, documents from the White House—as distinct from human sources—can aid an investigator.

The president and vice president, as politicians, must file documents with the Federal Election Commission. If a president is running for re-election by entering state primaries, he is eligible for public funds to match private contributions. To qualify, a candidate must raise $5000 in contributions of $250 or less from individuals in twenty different states. He must also agree to limit expenditures in each primary to an amount determined by the Federal Election Commission. Violations occur, and when they do, they are grist for investigators. In early 1981, the *New York Times* reported FEC auditors had determined that Reagan, while campaigning for the Republican nomination in 1980, exceeded the legal spending limit of $14.7 million. In the New Hampshire primary, the Reagan for President Committee was way above the $294,000 limit. Earlier, the FEC found the Carter campaign had topped spending limits in the Iowa, New Hampshire and Maine primaries.

In the general election (which begins after the parties nominate their candidate), private contributions to major party candidates are banned, except in specific circumstances. During the 1980 general election campaign, Reagan and Carter each received $29.4 million. Independent candidate John Anderson received $4.2 million after the election because he had received enough votes to be eligible for public money.

In addition to disclosing their campaign finances, the president and vice president must disclose their personal finances. The reports are due by May 15, as are the reports for other government officials covered by the law. To help avoid conflicts of interests, the president and vice president may put their assets into blind trusts. The Associated Press reported in early 1981 that the blind trust of George Bush and his wife totalled about $900,000; it consisted largely of stocks, bonds and other paper investments but excluded money in bank accounts and the Bush's two homes. President Reagan and his wife established a blind trust that was valued at about $740,000. Edward Pound of the *New York Times,* using figures from the blind trust, financial disclosure forms and other documents, estimated Reagan's net worth at $4 million.

Most of the documents an investigator uses have little to do with campaign or personal finances; rather, they involve government policy. Deakin of the *St. Louis Post-Dispatch* said he refers often to the president's annual State of the Union and budget messages. "They are a benchmark to use in evaluating how the president is performing. They contain the president's programs, and the explanations of those programs. If Congress adopts a law and the president claims victory, you can go back to the basic documents and see if the law is the same as what was set out by the president."

The White House is a much more centralized assignment than Congress. By using only four resources, an investigator can obtain almost every document released by the White House. The first resource is the White House press office itself. Investigators with access to it can pick up reams of paper within minutes after an official announcement is made. Investigators without access can pick up the same documents the next day at a room on the ground level of the New Executive Office Building. They can also call the White House clerk to obtain a quick answer on the status of bills awaiting presidential action, and other matters.

The second resource is the *Weekly Compilation of Presidential Documents,* available by subscription from the Government Printing Office, at minimal cost. The booklet is nearly exhaustive—categories include communications to Congress from the president, executive orders, bill signings, memorandums to federal agencies, letters, messages, telegrams, nominations, meetings with foreign leaders and speeches.

The other resources are the *Federal Register,* a daily government publication described in the next chapter, and the *Congressional Record,* described in the previous chapter.

For example, if the president announces an appointment to a government post, the press office will issue a release. The same announcement will eventually appear in the *Weekly Compilation of Presidential Documents.* If the nomination requires congressional approval, the president must submit the name to Congress, at which point it will appear in the *Congressional Record.* When the nomination is voted upon, the *Congressional Record* will carry the results.

Nominations do not normally appear in the *Federal Register.* But much else does—executive orders, memorandums, proclamations. When President Reagan decided to end building temperature restrictions imposed by Carter, his proclamation was published in the *Federal Register.* An investigator who rarely frequents the White House press office might have missed the news release about the change in government policy, but he would have seen the announcement in the *Federal Register* that arrived in the mail, probably the next day.

The units of the Executive Office of the President issue occasional reports and studies. An investigator desiring those on a timely basis must develop sources within each unit. The White House Office of Administration publishes quarterly guides to the publications of each unit; they are available to the public.

Cannon at the *Post* tries to keep up with one type of unofficial "document"—out-of-town newspapers. "They give you a different slant, a different point of view," he said. "I also try to watch television news on the networks, because the modern Presidency is geared to television."

One part of the federal government not at all geared to television coverage is the bureaucracy—the Cabinet departments and the various agencies. They are the subject of the next chapter.

"Didn't You Used To Be In The State Department?"

The Cabinet Departments and the Agencies

The belief is nearly unanimous that Washington correspondents do a superficial job covering federal agencies. Researchers and scholars also pay little attention to the agencies, especially when compared to Congress and the Presidency.

"The agencies are terribly undercovered, especially the regulatory agencies, and it's not getting better," says James Deakin, long-time Washington correspondent for the *St. Louis Post-Dispatch*.

Routine administrative proceedings are rarely perceived as news, although management of rates and routes for airlines, trucks and trains may affect the daily lives of far more people than some extensively reported presidential action or congressional hearing. In *The Washington Reporters* (a scientific study of the media here), Brookings Institution researcher Stephen Hess says about 85 percent of the correspondents agree that agency coverage is a problem. But few want what they perceive as the dull assignment of reading documents; so government agencies—some with budgets larger than many foreign countries—are covered almost exclusively by specialized newsletters of limited circulation. When the Associated Press or United Press International assigns a reporter to an agency, he has so many other institutions on his beat that coverage is superficial. Rarely examined is what an agency is not doing—even though that may be a bigger news story.

One problem of coverage is the tendency of reporters to think collectively about "the regulatory agencies" or "the Cabinet." In fact, the agencies have vast, diverse responsibilities; they are not a unified beat simply because each regulates something, or because each has Cabinet status. Nonetheless, each agency has characteristics in common with every other. This chapter will look at the similarities that are useful to investigators.

The Departments and Agencies: An Overview

The most sprawling of the government bureaucracies are the Cabinet departments. Each is headed by a secretary who is appointed by the president with Senate confirmation. The secretary can be removed at will by the president, as when President Carter shook up the Cabinet in the middle of his term.

In 1981, there were thirteen Cabinet departments. Their organization is complex. For example, as of 1980 the Agriculture Department had—in addition to the secretary—a deputy secretary, six assistant secretaries, one under secretary and other assorted high-ranking political appointees. The Agriculture Department comprised fourteen "offices," ten "services," three "administrations," two "corporations" and two "boards." No matter how obscure or insignificant they appear to be, these subdivisions are not ignored by the best investigators. James Risser, *Des Moines Register* Washington correspondent, interviewed Agriculture Department grain division officials in their office at a remote shopping center in a Maryland suburb of Washington. "I think it was the first time a news reporter had come to their offices in years," Risser said.

The interviews were an early step in Risser's series about corruption in agencies designated to inspect American grain exports. That series won Risser a Pulitzer Prize in 1976. I.F. Stone, another Washington investigator, wrote an expose of nuclear testing based partly on data obtained from a nearly ignored branch of the Commerce Department.

Most Cabinet departments perform some regulatory functions. For the most part, however, the departments—including Commerce and Agriculture—spend money to manage programs intended to help specific constituencies or individuals.

About sixty agencies—each with its own complex structure of bureaus and offices—fall under the heading "independent establishments and government corporations." Some, such as the Environmental Protection Agency, are led by a single administrator appointed by the president. Others, such as the Federal Trade Commission, are ruled by a group of appointees, with one designated as chairman. The appointees usually cannot be removed at the will of the president—they are named for specific terms and serve out those terms unless leaving voluntarily. Some independent establishments, such as the National Science Foundation, exist largely to dispense money. Others are mainly regulatory; the Federal Communications Commission is one of these. The FCC makes sure that broadcasters, and others under the commission's jurisdiction, obey the law.

Who Are These Bureaucrats Anyway?

In 1980, the government employed about 2.9 million civilians. Approximately 65 percent of the civilian workforce worked for either the Defense Department, Veterans Administration or Postal Service. Most of the Federal work force lived outside the Washington, D.C. area—about three-quarters of the workers were based in the states. The remaining 25 percent worked either in Washington or overseas.

The United States Directory of Federal Regional Structure, available from the Government Printing Office, lists key personnel at federal agency offices outside Washington. What goes on in these regional offices can be of great significance to an investigator. In *The New Muckrakers*, Leonard Downie Jr. of the *Washington Post* recounts how two *Miami Herald* reporters uncovered scandal in the office of then U.S. Senator Edward Gurney by looking into the operations of the Federal Housing Administration's Miami office.

Because every state has a significant cadre of federal and postal workers, people throughout the nation have a stake in government operations, particularly in personnel matters such as civil service reform or pay increase proposals. Every state also has a share of the approximately two million members of the armed forces; as a result, an investigator might want to educate himself about the civil service and military systems. The *Washington Post* and *Washington Star* publish daily columns and news stories about federal workers. Vivian Vahlberg, in the Washington bureau of the *Daily Oklahoman and Times*, writes regularly about actions affecting the bureaucracy; the federal government receives this attention because it is the second largest employer in Oklahoma.

Despite the rhetoric of politicians about the evergrowing number of bureaucrats, the number of federal employees has not changed much in the past few decades. (Many agencies are, however, increasing their use of outside consultants, a practice which effectively enlarges the federal work force.) What has indisputably changed is the character of the work force. The *Washington Post* reported that from 1960 to 1980, the number of engineers on the federal payroll jumped 50 percent; attorneys increased 100 percent; social scientists, psychologists and welfare workers, 230 percent; computer specialists, 600 percent. In short, the work force has become more specialized and better educated—in 1980, the government employed 30,000 more engineers than it did clerk-typists.

Such highly trained specialists can be knowledgeable sources. *Post* reporter Kathy Sawyer used as an example Dean Neptune, a biochemist with a Ph.D. who was employed at the Environmental Protection Agency. Neptune's job was to analyze the chemicals found in industrial wastes. He told

Sawyer: "We help decide which toxic pollutants [the EPA] might consider regulating."

Most career employees are assigned to one of eighteen grades—GS (for "general schedule") 1 through GS-18. At the start of 1981, the lowest ranking GS-1 earned $7210. A GS-18 would have earned $65,750, except that Congress was limiting top pay to just above $50,000 annually. The true policy makers and administrators are theoretically found in grades GS-16 and above. Many are part of the Senior Executive Service, approximately 8500 strong. Bureaucrats who join can be removed more easily for poor performance than other civil servants, but also are eligible for bigger raises. Some investigators say they have had good luck getting information from bureaucrats at Senior Executive Service levels. Other investigators say they generally get better information from lower-level workers. Over 60 percent of non-supervisory federal employees (most of them below grade 13) are represented by bargaining units. There are dozens of unions, though four predominated in 1981; the American Federation of Government Employees (AFL-CIO), National Treasury Employees Union, National Federation of Federal Employees and National Association of Government Employees.

"Management" includes not only high-level bureaucrats in each agency, but also the Office of Personnel Management—a separate entity formerly known as the Civil Service Commission. OPM is a good source of information for investigators trying to understand government-wide personnel policy, or trying to determine whether practices in any single agency are unusual.

Most lower-level federal workers got their jobs by taking standardized tests administered by OPM. About 150,000 competitive civil service jobs are filled each year from outside the government unless a hiring freeze is on. Top career bureaucrats are exempt from the test; their education and job experiences are evaluated instead. The approximately 500 presidential appointees who are not career bureaucrats are placed in one of five levels; the highest is Level I, which includes Cabinet secretaries. (Level I pay was $69,630 at the start of 1981. Pay in Level V was $50,112.) The assistant secretaries in these categories can make news. Spencer Rich of the *Washington Post* reported that, during the last days of the Carter administration, an assistant secretary of labor "began churning out millions of dollars in post-election job training grants." Rich used the Freedom of Information Act to obtain information on specific grants that were under scrutiny because of the way they were awarded. Below Level V there are about 1800 non-career departmental appointees paid at upper-GS levels. Although not officially presidential appointees, these personnel are often cleared by the White House staff.

One way to identify political appointees is from a book published once every four years by the House Post Office and Civil Service Committee. Its official title is *Policy and Supporting Positions*; it is referred to as the "Plum Book." The book lists political and policy making jobs that the president or his designee can fill without going through civil service red tape. The 1980 edition contained over 6000 names and was read avidly by members of the incoming Reagan administration. So intense was the interest that the *Washington Star* published names and salaries from the book.

An investigator delving into the backgrounds of political appointees has many resources to draw upon. Senate hearings sometimes reveal damaging information. Or occasionally the politics surrounding the nomination become so heated that the name is withdrawn before a hearing. Norval Morris suffered this fate; he was President Carter's choice to head the Law Enforcement Assistance Administration. Carter also withdrew the nomination of Theodore Sorenson to head the Central Intelligence Agency. An investigator will find, however, that most nominations are routinely approved. During 1980, the Senate confirmed 3811 of 3934 civilian nominations. Most of those unconfirmed were due to lack of time. Every one of nearly 66,000 military nominations was approved. As of 1981, no Cabinet nominee had been rejected by the Senate since 1959.

An investigator searching for background on a nominee should examine information submitted to the appropriate Senate committee. The Commerce, Science and Transportation Committee, for instance, uses a questionnaire that requests, from nominees, tax returns for the past three years, other financial disclosures required by law, a report from the general counsel of the agency to which the nominee is being appointed and answers to queries submitted by individual senators. An investigator might also find information about recent political activities and campaign contributions, plus admissions of potential conflicts of interests. In 1981, based on documents filed with the Senate, the *Washington Star* ran a story about Transportation Secretary-designate Andrew Lewis. The *Star* noted thirteen actual or potential conflicts that Lewis promised to remedy by selling stock or by removing himself from certain decisions.

Unlike the old days, presidential appointees are usually not political cronies. Donald Regan, the choice of Ronald Reagan for treasury secretary, had not been active in politics and differed with the president's advisors on a number of economic issues. The president had not met some of his Cabinet secretaries until a few days before announcing their appointments. An investigator will probably find that most nominees come from the academic world, a corporation, the legal profession or the federal bureaucracy. Some have inhabited all those realms.

Where Cabinet members come from sometimes is a clue to the policies they will try to implement. James Perry of the *Wall Street Journal* noted that Ronald Reagan's Cabinet was not from the liberal Eastern Establishment, "but it is Establishment all the same, proving there is a powerful center in the American political system that influences almost all of the nation's politics."

Whatever the Cabinet member's background, he is usually perceived as too easily influenced by the outside constituencies he is supposed to be overseeing. There are notable exceptions, but the rule has held in administration after administration. When Reagan chose John Block as his agriculture secretary, the *New York Times* reported the president was under pressure to select "an active farmer who believed in farm programs," a description that fit Block. What frequently happens is that a Cabinet member, supposedly the president's trusted agent, becomes the mouthpiece to the president from interrelated industries, interests and regions. John Ehrlichman, top domestic aide to President Nixon, put it this way: "We only see them at the annual White House Christmas party; they go and marry the natives." This tendency is one reason Jimmy Carter—and previous presidents—backed away from much-heralded plans for "Cabinet government."

Soon after his election, Ronald Reagan announced that his Cabinet members would be policy advisors. Whether Reagan will backslide from this version of Cabinet government is something investigators could look into.

Cabinet secretaries and other federal appointees may leave quickly, often re-entering the revolving door to take jobs with interest groups they dealt with while in the government. The *National Journal* each week chronicles the comings and goings in its "People" section. Such movement raises questions about whether the public interest is taking a back seat to personal interests in policy making. Questions of ethical compromises and conflicts of interests are raised. Financial disclosures are filed by appointed officials and career bureaucrats who are GS-16 or higher. Reports for the previous year must be filed by May 15. A new bureaucrat covered by the law has thirty days in which to file after starting work. When a person is nominated by the president for a job requiring Senate confirmation, the nominees must disclose financial information within five days.

Investigators desiring to see these reports generally must go to the agency where the person is employed. Within that agency, the designated "agency ethics official" will have access to the reports. That person is usually, but not always, in the general counsel's office.

Some disclosures must be made under other laws by bureaucrats. For instance, a careful reader of the *Congressional Record* one day in 1980 would have seen that the secretary of the interior supplied Congress with financial disclosures of employees having responsibilities under the Energy Policy and Conservation Act and the Mining in the Parks Act. A separate *Congressional Record* notice would have tipped off an investigator to political contributions of four persons nominated by President Carter to be foreign ambassadors. A law requires disclosures to help guard against wealthy citizens secretly "buying" ambassadorships.

Another type of conflict prohibited throughout the government is nepotism. Supposedly, no government official is permitted to hire or promote a relative. In 1980, a top-level bureaucrat in the Department of Energy resigned after an investigation concluded her efforts to have DOE hire her stepson appeared to violate nepotism rules; the *Washington Post* reported the incident in detail.

No problem is more ripe for examination by investigators, however, than the previously mentioned revolving door. The phenomenon is most noticeable when those swinging through to take jobs in the private sector are either former members of Congress or Cabinet secretaries; it also is widespread at lower levels, though not so noticeable there. A 1978 law designed to minimize the adverse effects of the phenomenon has been weakened by congressional amendment and agency regulations; nonetheless, its major provisions may be useful to the investigator. The Ethics in Government Act prevents certain officials who have left from representing anyone on a matter if they "personally and substantially" handled that matter before. The ban is a lifetime one. Briefer bans are also spelled out. But the loopholes created by amendment and regulation will probably allow the old ways to continue largely uncorrected. Specific exemptions from post-employment restrictions are written into other laws, thus greasing the revolving door even more. Energy Secretary Charles Duncan Jr. invoked "national interest" to legally waive a ban on awarding a contract to former Energy Department employees.

Investigators interested in post-employment conflicts need to keep tabs on bureaucrats who have left government, in order to determine who they are representing before federal agencies. (The Office of Government Ethics within the Office of Personnel Management has responsibility for overseeing post-employment regulations.) The investigator will find clues from time to time in documents. For example, every year the Defense Department supplies the Senate Armed Services Committee with a list of military retirees or former civilian employees who have taken jobs with defense contractors, and vice versa. The 1980 list indicated that 1623 government defense employees moving into private industry slots; seventy-nine shifted from the private sector to the Defense Department. Howie Kurtz of the *Washington Star,* working from internal FBI documents, reported an investigation of a Federal Aviation Administration official who had awarded a $3.2 million contract to Computer Sciences Corporation. The official supervised the contract for two years. On his last day in government, he extended the contract. The next day he was in the employ of Computer Sciences Corporation.

Units Common to the Departments and Agencies

Although every agency is unique, there are similarities useful when investigating the bureaucracy. The first is the public affairs office. Every Washington correspondent worries about being misled by government "flacks." But for an investigator unfamiliar with an agency, a public affairs professional can save time by helping to find the appropriate official to interview, or by locating the necessary document. Readers of agency news releases will begin to recognize names of the public affairs people. In the Energy Department, for example, releases discussing coal may be written by one person and releases about nuclear waste written by another. If a question is a general one about nuclear waste, it makes sense to call the public affairs officer who specializes in that topic.

Many public affairs offices publish lists of which employees specialize in which topics. For example, in 1980 the Department of Health and Human Services list included over 100 topics—in alphabetical order—followed by the name and phone number of the public affairs expert in that area. If a separate public affairs directory is unavailable, the agency telephone directory (every agency publishes one) will help. Other publications reveal key public affairs numbers. The annual *United States Government Manual*—the government-published bible of the executive branch—is one. Among those published privately, the *Federal Yellow Book* from The Washington Monitor Inc. and Carroll Publishing Company's *Federal Executive Directory* are perhaps the most comprehensive and up-to-date. In 1981 the *New York Times* ran a feature about Carroll Publishing and its massive task of trying to keep its directory current, especially during a change of administration. Still others are Bendix Corporation's *Directory of Public Information Contacts*, updated annually, and Hill and Knowlton's *Directory of Key Government Personnel*, updated every other year.

An agency news release can even be a tip-off to scandal. James Risser, Washington Bureau chief for the *Des Moines Register*, said his 1976 Pulitzer Prize for a series about corruption in the grain export trade began with "a short and blandly worded" release from the Agriculture Department. "The release announced the suspension of five grain inspectors in Houston because of their having been indicted by a federal grand jury for accepting bribes to certify that ocean-going ships were clean and acceptable for loading with grain to be shipped overseas," Risser said. "What struck me about the release was the fact that the inspectors, although federally licensed, were employees of a private inspection agency. . .It seemed likely to me that the [agency] was some sort of business group and might very well be made up of people in the grain and shipping businesses. If that were the case, the regulators and the regulated might, if effect, be the same people—a serious conflict of interest situation."

In addition to mailing releases, agencies have call lists of reporters interested in breaking news on a particular subject. Many agencies have recordings of news items; or they have special phone numbers to call for comments, quotations or complete stories that can be taped by broadcast stations for use on local newscasts.

Some Washington correspondents say they never consult public affairs personnel when investigating a sensitive topic. But many others disagree; they say they use such personnel until lied to or led astray. "The attitude and personality of the top person in the public affairs office can make all the difference in the world," said James Deakin of the *St. Louis Post-Dispatch.* "The bureaucrats take their cue from the top person, especially if he's close to the head of the agency." As of 1981, five Cabinet public affairs offices were headed by an assistant secretary—a presidential appointee requiring Senate confirmation. In other Cabinet departments and agencies, the top public affairs official was usually designated by the secretary or chairman, perhaps after White House clearance. Many of the appointees are former reporters who understand journalists and other investigators. They can be especially valuable if they used to cover the agency themselves. Other appointees had their training in public relations or advertising.

Public affairs offices in Cabinet departments are often decentralized, which is important to know for an investigator trying to locate the most informed source. For example, in 1980 the Interior Department's director of public affairs had his own staff of twenty, including twelve professionals. The operating budget was $825,000. However, there were 200 additional public affairs professionals in various division of Interior, half in Washington and half in the field offices. The Office of Surface Mining Reclamation and Enforcement, the National Park Service, the Bureau of Land Management, the Bureau of Indian Affairs each employed public affairs staffers who were only sometimes answerable to the top department public affairs person. Each subunit also had its own Freedom of Information Act officer who handled requests for documents. Some FOI officers are part of the public affairs staff; some are not.

The public affairs office can be more than a starting point for information; it can be the subject of an investigator's scrutiny. Some public affairs offices squander taxpayer dollars on movies intended to educate the public about the agency's mission. In fact, the movies may be nothing more than shameless promotion of the agency. In the 1970s this type of filmmaking became so widespread that Washington was dubbed "Hollywood on the Potomac." At least a dozen agencies spend money on advertisements in print and broadcast media; the ads are placed through private businesses. *Advertising Age* reported in 1980 that the Pentagon budget for advertising would top $144 million during 1981.

Numerous magazines, newsletters and other periodicals flow out of public affairs offices. Some are of high quality and extremely informative to the lay reader; others are not. What all the magazines have in common is that they are underwritten with taxpayer dollars. A private service, Infordata International Incorporated, issues a quarterly *Index to U.S. Government Periodicals* that lists more than 175 publications from over 100 agencies. An investigator might wish to determine who actually reads these periodicals and learn whether some are boondoggles.

Not even government investigators have been able to determine agency public relations spending, because most agencies fail to keep their books in a useful manner. Sometimes an investigator trying to get an overview of the government's public affairs machine is better off beginning with the public affairs officials' own organization, the National Association of Government Communicators.

Every government agency has employees whose job it is to build bridges to Congress. They do not call themselves "lobbyists," yet part of their mission is to persuade Congress that the agency they work for is doing a good job and entitled to more money to do an even better one. A large number of these congressional liaisons have learned the ropes on Capitol Hill as committee staffers or as lobbyists for private organizations. These liaisons to Congress can be excellent sources. They may be willing to discuss the prospects for legislation affecting their agency or to mention who in Congress is leading the drive for passage. They may reveal the chief opponents of the legislation or what might be the motives of the principals involved. Agencies receive information requests from Congress regularly. An investigator will often find useful information in the replies, which might be available from the congressional liaison. (If that channel is closed, an investigator should request the reply from the member of Congress or committee making the inquiry.) During the 96th Congress, for example, the Justice Department received over 3000 queries about its views on legislation. Because a Justice Department response indicating that a bill has constitutional problems might doom that bill forever, an investigator doing a thorough job should be aware of such reaction.

Federal law prohibits out-and-out lobbying by government officials. In 1980, *Congressional Quarterly Weekly Report* told of an attempt by Len Stewart, director of legislative affairs for the federal Office of Surface Mining, to kill a bill moving through Congress by enlisting the aid of environmental groups. After an opponent within the agency leaked Stewart's memos to Congress, the Office of Surface Mining warned its personnel that "certain forms of lobbying are illegal when pursued by a government employee in the course of official business—in particular, recommending that citizens urge Congress to defeat or enact a bill."

Although Congress is supposed to oversee agencies, in fact much legislation affecting an agency is drafted in-house, then presented to Congress by the liaison with a request for passage. Once the appropriate panel approves the bill, it may ask the agency liaison to help draft the committee report explaining the bill. Ward Sinclair of the *Washington Post* learned about the practice while researching a 1980 series on the budget of the National Institutes of Health. "Theoretically, Congress and the executive branch are separate and independent," Sinclair said. "But for years, the House appropriators have allowed the agencies to provide 'suggested' language for the reports, which explain the bills and direct the bureaucrats."

Budget and procurement offices within each agency can help investigators determine where the money comes from and where it is going. When the White House sends the overall budget to Congress every January, agencies make their financial officials available for questions at briefings. Information from agency budget officers is sometimes supplemented—or contradicted—by staffers in the White House Office of Management and Budget and by those in Congress' General Accounting Office who are assigned to monitor an individual agency full-time.

If an agency is spending an inordinate amount in the last month of the fiscal year to avoid appearing as if it does not need its entire congressional appropriation, an investigator might get a tip to that effect from a disgruntled budget official—or at least get confirmation from one after documenting what was going on. During 1980, numerous Washington correspondents wrote about year-end spending sprees, especially after the General Accounting Office and two congressional committees highlighted the problem in reports and hearings. As a result of the publicity, Congress prohibited some agencies from spending over 30 percent of their funds during the last quarter or more than 15 percent in any month of the last quarter without approval from the Office of Management and Budget. An investigator can consult financial officials to determine if an agency is adhering to those limits.

John Herbers of the *New York Times* learned that agencies sometimes spend money too slowly, instead of too fast. A 1980 article by Herbers reported that $100 billion in approved public works projects remained unspent because of government inefficiency. A $6 billion public works program designed to counteract the 1975 recession failed to reach full speed until 1978, "when the economy was entering an inflationary period, and was thus counterproductive," Herbers said. By following the buck, an investigator can determine if a program, ballyhooed when first instituted, is being implemented properly, or at all; the implementation of public policy too often remains untracked by the media and the public.

Inextricably tied to agency budgets is procurement of goods and services. Every day every government agency spends money for everything from paper clips to expensive studies by outside consultants, and though the potential for abuse accompanies every contract, few stories are written about them. That kind of information rarely comes in a news release, especially when a procurement program is riddled with fraud or is failing to meet its social goals of helping businesses owned by blacks, or whatever.

There are ways, though, for investigators to get a handle on the more than $100 billion spent annually for procurement. Lists exists. For instance, the Defense Department reports to the House Appropriations Committee about funds paid by prime contractors to subcontractors when the award tops $500,000. The Pentagon also publishes a compilation of contracts when the negotiated amount is above $10 million. Thomas Love of the *Washington Star* reported in 1980 that a major supplier admitted to the Pentagon that it had failed to test transistors before selling them to the government. "As a result," Love said, "government officials say the reliability of vital defense and space systems may be in jeopardy."

The details of procurement scams sometimes seem laughable until the investigator remembers that taxpayer money is involved. In 1981, syndicated columnist Jack Anderson reported how a 32-cent replacement part needed by the Marines for their training center in Cherry Point, N.C., wound up costing $114 because of hitches in the procurement process. Anderson's conclusion: "The government procurement system is designed to make large expenditures out of small ones."

In the 1970s, when newspapers led by the *Washington Post* got around to investigating the General Services Administration, remarkable stories appeared about the government's chief landlord and purchasing agent. Indictments and convictions followed. Then, in 1980, *Post* reporters Jonathan Neumann and Ted Gup delved into another part of the government procurement process—research and consulting contracts. They studied over 16,000 contacts advertised by government agencies in 1979, and learned that the government had spent over $9 billion for outside expertise. More than two-thirds of the contracts were awarded without competitive bidding. Thousands of the consultants' reports lay unexamined in warehouses; those that were finally read by government officials often turned out to be useless.

Many contracts were awarded under questionable circumstances, as the *Post* series noted again and again. Government officials who awarded and monitored contracts routinely accepted favors from contractors. In one case, the contractor lived with the government employee heading the office that supervised the contract. In another instance, a firm hired prostitutes for the senior government official who supervised the firm's troubled contracts. Neumann and Gup also demonstrated that the federal government awarded multi-million dollar contracts to oil and chemical companies for data used in regulating their own products. The traditional adversary relationship between regulators and private manufacturers had broken down, they said.

By looking through vouchers, the *Post* reporters learned that a Cabinet department paid consultant William Ewald $440 for work performed on Sept. 31, 1978; September does not have thirty-one days. By reading *Commerce Business Daily*— the official government publication advertising federal contract opportunities—Neumann and Gup found that the 33,000 copies published daily (at an annual cost of $550,000) are largely ignored by businesses. Why? In most instances, an agency had decided who would receive the contract before advertising the job.

While the *Post* series was running, a congressional hearing revealed the Department of Energy spent 87 per cent of its $11 billion budget for outside consultants. The agency's own 21,000 employees were doing almost none of its research work. Plenty of outside consultants—called the "Beltway bandits" because of their location near the highway circling Washington, D.C.—were ready to take on government jobs. Deborah Randolph of the *Wall Street Journal* said the Washington yellow pages showed 1400 consulting firms, compared to about 900 just five years before. "In collecting those fees, consultants do pretty much the same things that government employees do," Randolph said.

An investigator looking for information on specific contracts awarded to consultants has other alternatives than digging through every one. For example, the Senate Appropriations Committee requires the Health and Human Services Department to report all payments to consultants over $25,000. By making inquiries at federal repositories, an investigator can find a substantial portion of consultant reports. The main repository is the National Technical Information Service, part of the Commerce Department, which describes itself as "the central source of U.S. government-sponsored research by national and local governmental agencies, their contractors or grantees, or by special technical groups." The service has more than one million titles available. A twice monthly journal, *Government Reports Announcements and Index*, includes summaries of current research reports available through the service.

Sometimes the consultants to whom an agency awards money are former agency employees. *Broadcasting* magazine reported in 1980 that the Federal Communications Commission had paid $43,200 in consulting fees to Max Paglin, a former FCC general counsel and executive director. To learn whether an individual has current or past ties to an agency, an investigator can begin with the agency's personnel office.

In most agencies, there is an office designated to ferret out wrongdoing, including shady procurement and consulting practices. The office is that of the inspector general, or some other internal auditor. As of 1981, a total of sixteen agencies had inspectors general. They made the headlines when President Reagan asked for their resignations. Opponents of Reagan's move complained that politicizing the position would hurt its effectiveness. Howie Kurtz of the *Washington Star* said of the inspectors general, "Some of them have saved millions of dollars in areas from Medicaid fraud to government purchasing, while others have been criticized for not being aggressive enough."

The primary responsibility of inspectors general is to make sure agency money is being spent for the intended purposes. The basic orientation is financial. The acting inspector general at the National Aeronautics and Space Administration said in 1981 that the agency had "cases against nearly every contractor" who had participated in the space program.

Some inspectors general have established fraud and abuse hotlines for internal tipsters wanting to remain anonymous. A general purpose hotline at the General Accounting Office—an arm of Congress—received 25,000 allegations of fraud, abuse and waste in 1979-80, according to *Congressional Quarterly Weekly Report*. Complaints were passed along to departmental inspectors general. Although top government officials were encouraging tipsters to speak up in the public interest, the Office of Special Counsel—created to protect government employees who blew the whistle—was seriously hamstrung in 1980. Columnist Jack Anderson wondered whether budget and staff cutbacks resulted because "the mini-agency pursued its mandate vigorously—perhaps too vigorously." Because investigators cannot be sure of help from the Office of Special Counsel, they must try to locate whistle blowers themselves. Several Washington correspondents said they cultivate sources who recently have left an agency, hoping to gather names of dissidents still working there.

The general counsel's office keeps track of lawsuits brought by an agency and those filed against it. During 1980, the federal government was involved in about 34,000 civil cases as the plaintiff and in about 30,000 as the defendant, plus

30,000 criminal cases. An investigator might need to go elsewhere within an agency for details of an investigation, especially if no litigation has been filed. For example, at the Securities and Exchange Commission in early 1981, the Enforcement Division—separate from the general counsel—had about 200 staffers. When Jerry Knight of the *Washington Post* looked into a largely secret SEC investigation of the billionaire Hunt family of Texas, he learned that thousands of pages of documents relating to the family's transactions were in the hands of the Enforcement Division. Because the SEC (and other agencies) may have various divisions looking into wrongdoing, the general counsel is often the best place to start when beginning an investigation.

The general counsel is useful on matters other than investigations and litigation. As the Agriculture Department described the job: "The general counsel is the principal legal advisor to the secretary [of agriculture] and the chief law officer of the department." When Sheilah Kast at the *Washington Star* wanted to know the outcome of a dispute between the government and charities over the distribution of $4 million to help poor people pay heating bills, she talked to the Energy Department's general counsel. A sharp-eyed investigator would see that the Energy Department publishes its general counsel's legal interpretations in the *Federal Register*. The interpretations are requested by companies that do not want to run afoul of the department's regulations. Many other agencies publish legal opinions. Those of the Federal Election Commission are listed in its monthly newsletter. Because the opinions are usually requested by persons concerned that what they want to do might be illegal, the decisions can tip off an investigator to which practices are permissible and which are not.

Every agency collects thousands of pages of information each year. Much of it is distilled by statistical officers and staff economists. The resulting reports are dry, but within their pages are data often useful to investigators. The Government

Printing Office publishes the *Federal Statistical Directory*, which provides names "of key persons engaged in statistical programs and related activities." A catalog, *Governmental Periodicals and Subscription Services*, lists dozens of statistical publications available at little or no cost.

Statistical reports, research papers and other volumes are often available in little-used, out-of-the-way agency libraries staffed by professional librarians. An investigator looking into energy use can study publications like the *Monthly Petroleum Statistics Report* or *Residential Electric Bills in Major Cities*.

Not all agency documents, of course, consist merely of tables and graphs. Every agency collects information from the sectors over which it has jurisdiction. The information is filed in agency public reference rooms, among other places. The White House Office of Management and Budget keeps computerized records of the forms that many agencies use to collect data. (Armed with those computer records, five of my graduate student reporters compiled guides during 1979 to all information that might be of use to Washington correspondents covering the Federal Trade Commission, Federal Communications Commission, Nuclear Regulatory Commission, Food and Drug Administration and Securities and Exchange Commission. The guides are available from the Freedom of Information Center at the University of Missouri School of Journalism and have been excerpted in the *Investigative Reporters and Editors Journal* and in *The Quill* magazine. Any energetic investigator could compile similar guides for other agencies.)

Although most Washington correspondents ignore documents—preferring instead to rely solely on interviews—those who do scrutinize agency documents regularly tend to be among this city's top investigators. Steve Aug of the *Washington Star* is one documents-oriented investigator who is worried about the future. The trend toward deregulation will mean less information collection by the government. In 1981, many agencies were phasing out forms that previously had been useful to investigators.

Rulemaking by Government Agencies

Entire books have been written on how Congress makes a law. An entire book could also be written on the way in which an agency makes a regulation. The processes change, naturally, but those changes can be stories in themselves. In 1981 Clyde Farnsworth of the *New York Times* reported that President Reagan had ordered agencies "to list alternatives, together with their costs and benefits, in putting new regulations out for public comment." After that was done, an agency would "be required to pick the least costly way of achieving the regulatory objective," Farnsworth said.

Many agencies publish their own summaries of how they do business. The Federal Communications Commission, for example, has a two-page sheet called "How FCC Rules Are Made." A government publication, *The Federal Register—What It Is and How to Use It,* has an easy-to-follow section on the rulemaking process in general. What follows is an example of how the Office of Surface Mining developed regulations to implement a law passed by Congress. An investigator will note the various stages at which he might find useful information.

To implement the law on an interim basis, the agency published "initial regulations" in the daily *Federal Register* about four months after the law was signed by President Carter. The regulations took effect thirty days after publication. Private groups challenged the regulations in court; most of the package was eventually upheld. The agency then began to draft permanent regulations. In mid-1978, seven months after publication of the interim regulations, a draft of the proposed permanent regulations was sent to 2500 interested organizations. Six days of hearings in six cities were held. OSM made alterations as a result of the comments, publishing the revised proposed permanent regulations two months after the earlier draft had been unveiled. The agency gave interested groups seventy days to comment, more than the thirty required by law. At least 15,000 pages of remarks were received from about 500 sources. During the comment period, OSM invited over 100 experts to divide themselves into twenty-two task forces. The experts analyzed the comments and recommended changes in the proposed regulations. A few months after all comments were received, OSM published final regulations having the force of law.

Sometimes an agency issues a "notice of inquiry" rather than a "notice of proposed rulemaking." The notice is a request for information on a broad subject. Either kind of notice is usually assigned a docket number. As comments are received from the public or other government agencies, they are placed in the docket file. Almost every agency has a public reference room in which docket files can be examined.

After proposals are published, "ex parte" rules come into play. These rules govern communication between outside parties and agency commissioners during rulemaking. The rules are intended to prevent outside groups from secretly influencing presidentially appointed commissioners. Ex parte rules do not prohibit communication during a rulemaking, but try to insure that all communication is part of the public record. Kathleen Sylvester of the *Washington Star* reported on a 1980 FCC controversy over ex parte rules. The agency had loosened restrictions on communication between commissioners and outside parties during pending cases, but decided to continue its practice "of requiring commissioners to place into public files memoranda describing meetings," Sylvester said. At the Federal Trade Commission, notice of any meeting between the commissioners and outside parties to a rulemaking must be published in advance in the agency's weekly calendar. Verbatim transcripts or summaries of the meetings are available to the public upon request. Even information supplied to the commissioners by their staff must be disclosed if the facts relate to the merits of the rulemaking and are not already part of the record.

Most investigators focus, in their stories, on how long it takes for an agency to approve rules. But sometimes a story has a different angle—the difficulty, for example, of undoing rules that have already been implemented. Brooks Jackson of the

Wall Street Journal reported that it took the Department of
Housing and Urban Development four years to eliminate requirements that homebuilders supply bedroom closets and
towel bars in bathrooms. Jackson, issuing a warning to President Reagan, said his story was "a tale of how even such
modest deregulation as easing a few housing construction rules
can consume an entire political stint in the capital."

Some agencies do more than make rules—they act as
quasi-judicial bodies. Agency administrative law judges
preside in hearings comparable to the non-jury civil proceedings of full-fledged courts. The judges rule in disputes over
rate changes, license grants and benefit claims. As of 1981,
there were about 1200 law judges in about thirty agencies.
Washington Post legal writer Timothy Robinson called them the
nation's "hidden judiciary." If a party to a law judge's ruling
dislikes the outcome, he can take further steps within the agency. After those steps are exhausted, he can go to a federal court
where the agency might be overruled.

An investigator looking for constraints on agencies should
check Congress as well as the courts. Use of the "legislative
veto" has increased in recent years. Congress has not armed
itself with across-the-board veto power of executive branch actions but, in 1980, the Congressional Research Service found at
least 167 laws with one or more congressional veto provisions.
About one-fourth of those laws were enacted during Jimmy
Carter's presidency. One type of veto allows either the House
or the Senate to block a rule by approving a resolution within a
fixed time after the agency's action. Another type of legislative
veto requires agency actions to be blocked by both the House
and Senate.

One part of administrative decision making overlooked by
too many investigators is the advisory committee. Granted,
sometimes advisory groups play no role in decision making,
serving instead as window dressing. But if a useless advisory
body still exists, that fact should be of interest to an investigator as an example of government waste. Many groups,

however, are not just window dressing. A classic example was profiled in a 1960 *Harper's* magazine article by Hobart Rowen, currently of the *Washington Post*. Rowan called the Business Advisory Council of the Commerce Department, a tight fraternity of about 160 business executives, "one of the most exclusive clubs in the United States."

Two decades later, Kenneth Bredemeier of the *Post* profiled a very different, yet nonetheless influential, advisory group—the Commission of Fine Arts. Bredemeier called the group "a little-known band of seven Presidential appointees who, with a modest budget and no legal powers, exercise extraordinary influence on the appearance and shape" of Washington D.C.

Advisory groups are supposed to self-destruct every two years unless officially rechartered. Few ever die. They are governed by the Federal Advisory Committee Act, which, among other things, contains provisions for balanced representation and public meetings. In 1979, the Committee Management Secretariat of the National Archives and Records Service identified 820 advisory committees. The secretariat's *Federal Advisory Committee Annual Report*, conveniently alphabetized, is perhaps the most complete source of groups easily available to an investigator. The secretariat places advisory committees into these categories: those specifically mandated by Congress in a law, those allowed under an agency's jurisdiction by congressional approval, those established under the agency's general authority and those established by presidential executive order. The *New York Times* reported in 1981 that President Reagan was thinking of abolishing some advisory groups, but would probably retain them to reward his supporters with appointments.

The *United States Government Manual* lists a variety of federal boards, commissions and other bodies that do not fall under the jurisdiction of the Federal Advisory Committee Act. Although these groups are obscure, they can be useful to investigators interested in delving into specific topics—for example, the Committee on Foreign Investment in the United States, the Endangered Species Commission, the National Commission on Air Quality, and many more.

Keeping Track of What's Happening in the Agencies

The *Federal Register* is the most valuable government-wide tool for investigators interested in the departments and agencies, just as the *Congressional Record* is the best starting point for correspondents on Capitol Hill. The *Federal Register* is available by subscription from the Government Printing Office every weekday, except legal holidays. The cost in 1981 was less than 50 cents an issue—a bargain. The *Register* is well-indexed; an investigator wanting to keep tabs on just one agency can do so easily. The Office of the Federal Register sponsors workshops in Washington, D.C. and elsewhere on how to use publication. The *Register* of January 19, 1981, was the thickest ever—1191 pages of closely spaced type, or approximately 4600 manuscript pages. Philip Hilts of the *Washington Post* explained the extraordinary size of the volume by noting that the Carterites would be out, and the Reaganites in, the next day. "Before the change of administration," Hilts said, "agency officials want to see in place as many rules and programs as they can, to finish projects they have started and leave their mark on government after they depart."

A particularly valuable tool published in the *Register* is an agency's semi-annual agenda of regulations. The agenda describes what the agency is planning to investigate during the next six months, when the examination might be completed and who in the agency can provide additional information. Also during 1980, the U.S. Regulatory Council twice used the *Register* to publish a listing of significant pending items. The November version, 414 pages long, provided information about major regulations under development at thirty-eight departments and agencies. When, in early 1981, the council published a separate comprehensive list of rules affecting the automobile industry, Sheilah Kast of the *Washington Star* said the report "could become a 'hit list' for regulation-cutters in the new [Reagan] administration."

Investigators tracking the agencies should use the *Federal Register* in conjunction with the *Congressional Record*. The bureaucracy is required by law to submit thousands of reports every year to Congress. Those reports might not show up in the *Register*, but appear instead in the *Record's* executive communications sections for the House and the Senate. During the 1981 debate over American aid to El Salvador, an investigator would have found this item buried in the fine print of the House executive communications section of the *Congressional Record*: a letter from the secretary of state to the Foreign Affairs Committee, "transmitting notice of the president's intention...to authorize the furnishing of certain emergency military assistance to El Salvador."

To supplement the *Record* and the *Register*, an investigator can consult in-house agency publications, as well as specialized periodicals put out by independent businesses or special interest groups that focus on specific bureaucracies. Agency telephone directories are helpful, too. One Washington correspondent said he keeps agency directories for at least five years. "That enables me to determine which bureaucrats have been with the agency for awhile, and which have departed," he said. "Those who have left might talk more freely, or tap me into the malcontents who have stayed."

Of all the agencies, the State Department and Defense Department are the most prestigious journalistically. They are covered regularly by more reporters than any other federal entity. But the quality of the coverage is often criticized. In his book *Investigative Reporting*, Clark Mollenhoff says that "the ineffective and superficial coverage of the Pentagon continues to be the sorriest story in Washington."

The State Department

At the State Department, about 500 reporters were accredited in early 1981. More than half were from foreign countries. Passes from the congressional galleries are not honored at the State Department, but White House passes are. Investigators can receive clearance for department events without accreditation, but having a card avoids hassles and saves time. A letter from the employer is needed for accreditation, but even self-employed stringers can obtain accreditation from the public affairs office. The State Department Correspondents Association decides on its own membership, but does not have the power to accredit journalists. That power resides with State Department officials. In early 1981, the association was headed by a Reuters reporter. The department's press room on the second floor of the main building at 21st and C streets Northwest is occupied by department regulars. State Department public affairs officials are available for questioning one corridor away. Valuable information can be obtained in the press room and at the daily briefing for reporters.

Reading what various correspondents write about the State Department is useful. Not all the tips are in specialized publications, either, although it certainly makes sense to read respected independent journals such as *Foreign Policy, Foreign Affairs* and *Orbis. The New Yorker,* for example, ran a three-part series by Robert Shaplen in 1980 on David Newsom, undersecretary of state for political affairs. From that series, an investigator could have learned potentially useful tidbits. Important incoming cables and intelligence reports from all over the world were routed first to Newsom's office, Newsom was directly involved in naming American ambassadors to foreign nations and was supposed to find blacks and other minorities to work in the department.

The secretary of state, Newsom's boss, was of course much more visible than Newsom. Most secretaries hold periodic news conferences. For reporters who cannot attend, a transcript is available from the State Department. During the Carter administration, Secretaries of State Edmund Muskie and Cyrus Vance held Friday afternoon background briefings for regular State Department reporters in the secretary's office, sometimes over drinks; questions were answered on a not-for-attribution basis.

Attending daily briefings given by the secretary's press officer is another way to learn the official line. Francis Cline of the *New York Times* called the briefing "one of the toughest daily forums in the capital. . .Journalists who have covered other parts of Washington feel that the State Department briefing is better than any other forum, notably the White House and Pentagon, as a source of articles and an area for relatively studious questioning."

A daily appointments schedule of the secretary and his top aides is a useful supplement to the daily briefing. On one day in 1980, the appointments schedule showed Muskie meeting in succession with the Italian foreign minister, the Philippines' foreign minister, the assistant secretary for international organization affairs and the Congresswomen's Caucus. Newsom was meeting with the Romanian deputy foreign minister, the vice president of Botswana and the Finnish undersecretary for foreign affairs. Another high-ranking State Department official was testifying before a House Appropriations subcommittee.

Some State Department reporters gather information by waiting in the main lobby to collar officials and their foreign visitors. While waiting, a reporter can read the official documents that abound, such as news releases from the public affairs office, Background Notes on individual foreign nations and position papers on such topics as U.S.-Chinese relations. The monthly *Department of State Bulletin* is a magazine that compiles speeches, actions on treaties and more into a handy package. Daily reports on various areas of the world are available from the Foreign Broadcast Information Service. Each report contains current news and commentary monitored by FBIS from foreign broadcasts, news agency transmissions, newspapers and periodicals. The State Department public affairs office distributes at least 300 publications on a regular basis.

The Pentagon

At the Defense Department, regular reporters have a building pass issued at the discretion of public affairs officers in the Pentagon. The pass allows journalists to go into the building at a number of entry points. Press passes from the congressional galleries, White House and State Department are honored. A non-regular who expects to be visiting the Pentagon frequently to do one story can get a temporary building pass, valid for three months. A letter of introduction is helpful in obtaining such a pass. An investigator can gain entry by calling ahead on a one-time basis, but somebody from the press section will have to meet him in the concourse and escort him to his destination. There is an area set aside for journalists in the "E" ring; this area is called the "Correspondents' Corridor." Nearby are the desks and offices of public affairs personnel for the secretary of defense. Public affairs officers for the individual military services are scattered throughout the building.

The secretary of defense traditionally holds periodic news conferences. Transcripts are available afterward. Regularly scheduled news briefings, conducted by a public affairs officer, are also available in transcript form for investigators. As in any Cabinet department, investigators have numerous one-time and periodic reports to choose from. At Defense, some of the most useful reports are the annual posture statements of the secretary and the chairman of the Joint Chiefs of Staff, quarterly reports on arms strength and enlistments, monthly reports on the progress of weapons systems and news releases listing contract awards. Branches of the military publish their own magazines (such as the Navy's *All Hands*). Much of the material is fluff, but even amidst fluff many leads can be pinpointed.

There is no hard-and-fast rule regarding those times an investigator should rely on department-wide sources, as opposed to relying on those in a particular service (Army, Navy, Air Force, Marines). When in doubt, an investigator should probably begin by calling the assistant secretary of defense for public affairs, or the directorate for defense information under the assistant secretary's jurisdiction.

Just as with the State Department, independent specialized publications are valuable resources. *Aviation Week and Space Technology, Aviation Daily* and *Armed Forces Journal* are but a few. For investigators unable to keep up with the specialized publications, a shortcut is the Defense Department's "Current News," a daily clip sheet of articles about national security and foreign affairs. The August 1, 1980, edition contained twenty-two articles from over a dozen publications. A companion Defense Department sheet is called "The Friday Review of Defense Literature." It briefly describes major articles, research papers and books.

Again, human sources must be stressed. Any good investigator will make as many contacts as he can inside a department. He will have the most up-to-date departmental telephone directory. He will also cultivate sources outside the department. In the case of defense topics, that means members of Congress and their staffs, especially those on the authorizing and appropriations committees dealing with defense, national security and foreign affairs. It also means officials in other parts of the executive branch who share jurisdiction with the Defense Department—for example, sections of the State Department, the White House National Security Council and the International Communication Agency; defense experts outside government, at think tanks like the American Enterprise Institute for Public Policy Research and the Rand Corporation; lobbyists for defense contractors; and Washington representatives of various public interest groups promoting peace or stronger defense capabilities.

Much of what government agencies try to do is challenged in federal courts by aggrieved parties. The courts are the subject of the next chapter.

The Supreme Court and the Lower Federal Courts

I nvestigative reporters Bob Woodward and Scott Armstrong, in their book *The Brethren*, say "virtually every issue of significance in American society eventually arrives at the Supreme Court." These issues, though not necessarily of national significance, often have great impact on a geographic area, a particular industry or a specific group such as women or blacks. Yet each year hundreds of cases are decided or rejected by the Court in what is nearly a void, so far as public knowledge is concerned. Considering that there are thousands of reporters in Washington, D.C., it is suprising how few track the Supreme Court consistently.

Why is the Supreme Court so sporadically covered? One reason is that Washington correspondents view it as an undesirable beat—many hours reading legal briefs, few sources to interview, few scoops because upcoming rulings are closely guarded, little travel and less-than-prominent play for most stories.

Obtaining access to the Court building is easy—no accreditation is necessary to enter it or to use the media facilities on the ground level. The thirty to forty regular Supreme Court reporters, however, are on a list compiled by the court's public information officer allowing them to enter the building when it is closed to the general public. Another privilege for "regulars" is automatic seating for oral arguments in the Supreme Court chamber; there is a special section reserved for journalists. Any journalist with identification can request a pass (on a one-time basis) to sit in that section. About thirty-five seats are normally available, though media seating can be expanded for major cases. The public information office issues the passes.

Although gaining access to the Court building is relatively easy, determining what the Court is doing takes initiative; secrecy is the watchword. "The Court's deliberate process—its internal debates, the tentative positions taken by the justices, the preliminary votes, the various drafts of written opinions, the negotiations, confrontations and compromises—is hidden from public view," note Woodward and Armstrong.

There are no inside sources in the traditional sense—only documents, and Court employees who will help locate those documents. The staff of the public information office on the ground floor of the Court building is often helpful, but they generally limit themselves to answering questions of procedure, not of substance.

Investigators, however, can help themselves by knowing certain details. For example, an investigator following a case from a lower court to the Supreme Court should keep count of the days: an appeal in a criminal case is not timely unless it has arrived in the Supreme Court clerk's office within sixty days of the decision. In a civil case the appeal must be made within ninety days.

Because there are so few sources inside the Supreme Court, investigators must try to develop outside ones. The lawyers who file briefs in a case can be interviewed. Sometimes it is wise to interview the actual litigants: Supreme Court cases consist of real people who are charging wrongdoing or who are accused of wrongdoing. Fred Barbash *Washington Post* Supreme Court reporter, said, "There are human beings behind those briefs. They're non-intelligible as pieces of paper. I want to put flesh and blood into them."

Some Supreme Court reporters keep files of potential sources uninvolved in a given case—constitutional law experts at universities; subject matter specialists willing to comment, for example, about what a decision on converting utilities to coal will mean to the environment; or procedural experts within groups that litigate a lot, such as the American Civil Liberties Union. "Lawyers usually haven't read the opinion by the time I have to write," says Knight-Ridder's Aaron Epstein, an award-winning Supreme Court reporter. "So I build up experts who will react and analyze on the basis of what I say."

The nine justices almost never grant interviews. Nonetheless, an investigator can learn about them. Background knowledge about the justices sometimes helps explain a case's outcome. The justices are human, and there is evidence in their own writings that rulings are sometimes based as much on emotion as on law. Having background knowledge about a justice might also help an investigator understand a particular justice's role in Court politics, the kind of maneuvering portrayed in *The Brethren*.

The Woodward-Armstrong book, released at the end of 1979, taught readers a great deal about the justices, but it has made uncovering information even more difficult; after *The Brethren* was published the justices and Court personnel became more guarded when dealing with outsiders. It is no secret what types of sources Woodward and Armstrong used for much of their information: several justices, about 170 former law clerks, former Court employees, unpublished documents and published opinions. (Woodward and Armstrong promised confidentiality to most sources, however.) So, today's investigator may have a tough time, but the task is not impossible.

To learn about a justice, an investigator can examine what he was doing before his appointment to the Court. Standard biographies are a place to start. If the justice was a lower court judge, how did he perform there? Interviews with lawyers and litigants who appeared before him can be enlightening. Former law clerks and legal secretaries might be willing to talk. Clerks of court and other administrative support personnel might reveal information or insights. A review of the opinions written, combined with a study of how often the judge was reversed on appeal, often paints an interesting picture.

Even if the justice did not sit as a lower court judge, he studied, taught or practiced law somewhere. What was his reputation among his colleagues? Among his clients? Some justices have served in other branches of government. Chief Justice Warren Burger was a U.S. assistant attorney general; so was William Rehnquist. Byron White was a U.S. deputy attorney general. Thurgood Marshall was on the other side of the Supreme Court bench for three years as solicitor general. John Paul Stevens was a subcommittee counsel in the U.S. House. How did these men function in those jobs? Many justices have been involved in partisan politics—learning about those activities might be revealing. The transcripts of a justice's confirmation hearing in the U.S. Senate probably contains information about previous jobs, financial holdings and judicial philosophy.

Supreme Court justices must file financial disclosure statements each May with the ethics committee of the Judicial Conference of the United States. The easiest access to the statements, however, is at the Supreme Court public information office. As of early 1981, the chief justice's salary was $92,400 annually. The associate justices received $88,700. Lower court judges are paid less, but also receive hefty amounts.

By studying the financial disclosure forms, Gil Cranberg, editorial page editor of the *Des Moines Register*, learned that Justice Potter Stewart and the wife of Justice Lewis Powell owned stock in Johnson & Johnson. During 1980, the Court said it would not review a case involving a Johnson & Johnson subsidiary. The failure to review worked to the benefit of the subsidiary. It takes four justices to order a review. Consider: If Stewart and Powell did participate in the decision to allow review, they had an apparent conflict of interests. On the other hand, if they withdrew from the discussion, the withdrawal meant the company opposing Johnson & Johnson was at a disadvantage in that it needed four of seven votes rather than four of nine. But Court personnel refused to say whether the two justices participated. The *Register* editorialized that the secrecy was inexcusable. The paper said it was forced to conclude that the justices might have violated federal law as well as the Code of Judicial Conduct.

An investigator can look elsewhere for insight into a justice's background and thinking. Sometimes the justices give speeches; transcripts are available at the Court's public information office. When Chief Justice Burger said that his 1981 speech to the American Bar Association convention would be "a blockbuster," he was correct if the next day's headlines were any indication. Reporters covering the speech even got an unusual story beforehand when the normally distant chief justice spoke informally to newspeople at the convention. Lyle Denniston of the *Washington Star,* the dean of Supreme Court reporters, found the incident worthy of a feature; it ran under the headline "Burger Ends Coolness to the Press/Chief Justice Makes Pitch for ABA Talk."

An internal newsletter called "The Docket Sheet" is issued six times a year. It contains a column about the doings of the justices outside the job. For example, an investigator interested in knowing more about Justice Stevens would have learned from the newsletter that the *Chicago-Kent Law Review* published a tribute to the justice, and that an article by Stevens ran in the *Arizona Law Review.*

Following a Case Through the Supreme Court

The first thing an investigator needs to understand is how cases come to the Supreme Court. Not just any case is eligible for consideration. About 4800 civil and criminal petitions were filed in the 1979-80 term after decisions were handed down in lower state and federal courts. The Supreme Court also has original jurisdiction—specified in the Constitution—in a handful of cases stemming from certain types of disputes, such as those between states or between a state and the federal government. If questions of fact are in dispute in a case accepted under the court's original jurisdiction, the justices may name a "special master" to conduct a hearing.

Litigants almost always request the Supreme Court to take a case by granting either a petition of appeal or a writ of certiorari. A party filing an appeal believes it has a right to Supreme Court consideration. The legal right can exist under several conditions; a typical one is a state supreme court ruling that a federal law is unconstitutional. Still, cases on appeal are not guaranteed hearings by the Supreme Court. The Court might deny review "for want of a substantial federal question" or some similarly worded phrase. All the investigator can do then is infer that four justices could not be convinced to hear the case on its merits. One study noted that, over a number of years, only 15 percent of appeals were accepted for argument on the merits of the case.

A writ of certiorari claims no right to be heard. Rather, the lawyers ask the Supreme Court to exercise its discretion and grant the plea that the case be heard. One study revealed that only about 13 percent of writs of certiorari were granted. Most cases in which review is granted are set for oral argument, with a full decision eventually issued. Some cases accepted by the Court, however, are decided without oral argument or a full-length opinion. The lower-court decision may be summarily affirmed, reversed, or vacated (an action which could lead to a new trial). A special category of writ of certiorari fares worse still: petitions from indigents, usually prisoners. One study indicated that pauper petitions were granted review less than 5 percent of the time. Lawrence Baum, in his book *The Supreme Court*, cited a 1 percent acceptance figure for pauper cases.

The statistics from 1979-80 tell a revealing story: The Court looked at 2509 paid cases and 2249 pauper cases. Review was granted in 199 paid cases. Of those, 124 were set for oral argument. The other seventy-five were summarily decided. Of all the pauper cases, thirty-two were set for oral argument and forty-nine were summarily decided. The remainder were not considered by the Court.

At least some of the screening was done by law clerks. Each justice is allowed to employ four. They are generally top graduates of law schools. Some justices rely heavily on law clerks for screening cases, other justices do not. Each justice eventually decides which pending petitions he would like the Court to consider on the merits. But no case is accepted for consideration unless at least four justices approve. The point is this: Of all cases appealed to the Supreme Court, most are never considered. If a case is important to an investigator, he will have to learn whether the court has refused the case. If it is refused, the lower-court decision probably remains in effect and becomes the law.

So, it is time to return to square one. If a court case is important to an investigator, he probably will know about it before it reaches the Supreme Court. His bosses outside Washington may have told him they expect an appeal. He may know an appeal is imminent from reading newspapers, magazines or newsletters, or from listening to the broadcasts that are part of his routine. Perhaps a lawyer in the case has tipped him off.

All is not lost, however, if an investigator fails to hear about an important appeal ahead of time. He can still look at petitions as they are shelved in the Court's public information office. Or he can subscribe to a service such as *U.S. Supreme Court Bulletin* of Commerce Clearing House Inc. or *The United States Law Week* of the Bureau of National Affairs. Each service lists every request for a hearing filed at the Court. The public information officers will make these publications available for use on the Court's premises. John Fogarty, *San Francisco Chronicle* reporter, uses the publications as tools to determine if a case is particularly interesting to his newspaper. "To regionalize, I look for the circuit (from which the case is being appealed), and then try to narrow it within the circuit to

Northern California by looking a the lawyers involved," he said.

James O'Shea, who covered the Court for the *Des Moines
Register* before moving to the *Chicago Tribune,* tried to find
Iowa angles in non-Iowa cases. "I remember looking at a case
involving a Wisconsin trucking company and realizing that if it
were decided a certain way, it would possibly overturn Iowa's
controversial ban on long trucks," O'Shea said.

After learning that a newly filed case is of interest, an investigator should read the briefs and take notes in advance to
avoid the crush on decision days, when access to briefs is difficult. A call to the lawyers might help clarify murky areas.
After that, there is nothing to do but wait. Once or twice a week
when the Court is in session, the justices hold a closed-door conference. As much as six weeks before the conference, it is
possible to obtain a list of cases (by number only) that are expected to be discussed. Journalists generally refrain from
writing stories based on the conference list, but at least have
the notice they need that a case is about to be accepted for
argument, or rejected.

The justices issue an orders list after a conference is concluded. It is posted in the public information office at 10 a.m.
the first day of the week that the justices are on the
bench—usually Monday. If the list shows a case will not be
heard, the lower-court decision may be the new law. Sometimes
denial of a writ of certiorari is accompanied by a dissenting opinion from one or more justices in which they explain why they
would have granted review.

If the Court agrees to hear a case on its merits, additional
briefs will be filed. The party bringing the case has forty-five
days to submit its briefs; reply briefs are due thirty days later.
Supreme Court rules set out a standardized organization for
briefs. After reading a few, an investigator begins to learn
where to look for the important points.

Eventually, oral argument is scheduled. It occurs, on the
average, three to four months after the Court announces it will
hear a case. Each side is usually allotted thirty minutes to present its points. Additional time might be granted by the justices

upon advance request. The oral argument is heard in open court. The justices are seated by seniority, with the chief justice in the center, the senior associate justice to his right, the second most senior associate justice to his left, and so on back and forth. The justices can, and do, break in with questions at any time.

Colleen Davis, a graduate student in journalism when she interviewed fourteen Supreme Court reporters for a 1979 research project, comments that "only a few reporters attend oral arguments with any frequency. Most say their only benefit is to give a reporter an idea of which way the justices are leaning. Occasionally, as in the reverse discrimination cases of Allan Bakke and Brian Weber, oral arguments are events in themselves, generating their own news stories."

If the U.S. government is involved in the case, the lawyer appearing for it probably will be the solicitor general or a member of his staff. Only a few federal agencies are allowed to take cases to the Court without the solicitor general's consent. The solicitor general chooses cases carefully for submission to the Supreme Court; he knows that the justices will reject most requests for a hearing. Wade McCree Jr., solicitor general under President Carter, said many government losses in lower courts are never appealed. (Sometimes there are disagreements between the solicitor general and a government agency about whether to appeal. In 1980, the secretary of health and human services asked the government to halt filing a petition to the Supreme Court because the views of that Cabinet department were being presented inadequately. Lyle Denniston of the *Washington Star* wrote about the dispute after obtaining a private letter from HHS Secretary Patricia Harris to Attorney General Benjamin Civiletti.) McCree said his selectivity made sense. He noted that only 6 percent of all petitions for certiorari had been granted by the Supreme Court in 1979, but, in contrast, 72 percent of the government's sixty-eight petitions were granted.

After oral arguments are completed, a transcript is made. It is available in the public information office about a week later, but the names of the justices asking the questions are deleted. Soon after oral arguments, usually the same week, the justices discuss in a secret conference what they have read and heard. They speak in turn, by seniority, with the chief justice going first. Once the justices have decided whether to affirm or reverse the lower court, an opinion must be issued. If the case is a simple one, a per curiam opinion might be released. It is unsigned and brief. Quite often, it represents the views of a unanimous court.

If a full opinion is to be issued, though, it is assigned to a member of the Court by the chief justice—if the chief is in the majority. He can, of course, assign the opinion to himself—and often does in highly publicized cases or in cases of unusual legal interest. If the chief is in the minority, opinion assignment is handled by the most senior justice in the majority. An opinion is drafted and circulated among the members. Changes are often suggested, and the majority opinion writer sometimes incorporates the suggestions into his opinion. Other justices in the majority might write concurring opinions, indicating that they agree with the result but disagree with the reasons stated. Justices in the minority might issue dissenting opinions. Some decisions are announced just days or weeks after the oral argument, though it is common for months to go by between the time of the argument and the announcement. Leaks are rare, but not unprecedented. ABC-TV reporter Tim O'Brien breached court security in 1979 by obtaining advance information on cases involving libel and inmate paroles. O'Brien aired the gist of the opinions before they were released by the Supreme Court.

The text of opinions, with concurrences and dissents if any, is available in the public information office. A one or two-page syllabus summarizes the opinion. The syllabus also shows at a glance from which lower court the case came, the date the case was argued before the Supreme Court, which justice delivered the majority opinion, who joined it, which justices delivered concurrences and which dissented. If a justice did not take part in the case, that is noted, too, although the explanation is omitted. It is almost impossible for an investigator, however resourceful, to learn why a judge excused ("recused" in legal language) himself. An unusual recusal occured in late 1980 in a case about whether Congress acted wrongly when rolling back pay raises for federal judges. Justice Harry Blackmun took his name off an opinion after hearing the oral arguments and listening to discussion among the justices, according to a story by Denniston of the *Washington Star*. As always, there was no explanation from Blackmun or court staffers.

An investigator trying to keep track of numerous cases can relax somewhat during July, August and September. There are always cases to follow, but the justices slow their pace during this time; some get away for extended vacations. The new Court term opens on the first Monday in October. Oral arguments are usually heard on Mondays, Tuesdays and Wednesdays, during seven two-week periods stretching into May. Cases are generally heard from 10 a.m. to noon and from 1 to 3 p.m. During oral arguments weeks, conferences are held on Friday and sometimes Wednesday. Recesses alternate with the two-week sittings. During the recesses, the justices write opinions and take care of business brought to the Court. Oral arguments and conferences are not held; opinions are not delivered. A thorough investigator might use these slower times to find out whether the court's decisions are being implemented. The Supreme Court (like lower courts) has few means of assuring that what it orders will be carried out. School desegregation is a prime example.

Lower Federal Courts

For an overview of all the courts in the federal judiciary, a useful book is the *United States Court Directory*, available from the Government Printing Office. The directory lists judges and their office telephone numbers, plus names of such court staffers as the clerk and the librarian.

The court just below the Supreme Court is the U.S. Court of Appeals. There are eleven in the nation (twelve as of October 1, 1981). But the appeals court for the District of Columbia is of special interest to investigators based here. Like every other circuit, the D.C. circuit is overseen by a Supreme Court justice. But the day-to-day caseload is handled by appeals court judges appointed for life by the president with the consent of the Senate. The D.C. circuit had a chief judge and ten circuit judges at the start of 1981. Cases are usually heard by a three-judge panel. Occasionally, all the judges sit together to hear attorneys argue a case.

Most journalists wait until the appeals court has issued a decision before preparing a story. But some find cases interesting enough to write about while the cases are pending. Thomas Love of the *Washington Star* did that in 1980, chronicling a dispute between a District of Columbia shipping company and the Commonwealth of Puerto Rico, The Justice Department had intervened in behalf of Puerto Rico, saying the commonwealth was immune from the alleged antitrust violations charged by the shipping company.

In 1980, about 1600 appeals were filed in the D.C. circuit, about half of them from government agency administrative proceedings. By law, some agency decisions go directly to the appeals court, bypassing the U.S. District Court. In the D.C. circuit, the bulk of the administrative appeals came from the Federal Communications Commission, Federal Energy Regulatory Commission and Interstate Commerce Commission. Rulings are available in the clerk's office, which is located on the fifth floor of the federal courthouse, Constitution Avenue and John Marshall Place Northwest, at the foot of Capitol Hill. Calendars of hearing and other informative bulletins are posted in the clerk's office across from the door. There is little self-service; someone wanting to look at a case file will have to ask for it at the counter and wait until it is brought to him. Appeals court judges are generally unapproachable; their law clerks generally are not helpful, either.

The U.S. District Court for Washington (there are ninety federal district courts nationwide) is also in the federal courthouse, and takes up much of the second, fourth and sixth floors. At full strength, the court has a chief judge and fourteen district judges appointed for life by the president with consent of the Senate. (As with appeals court judges, senators may have a say in suggesting nominees when vacancies occur on the bench.) District court is a trial court where lawyers and witnesses appear before a judge and sometimes a jury. The U.S. attorney for the District of Columbia is a presidential appointee. He or his assistants handle cases on the government's behalf. Other officers of the court who might be of assistance to investigators are the clerk, magistrates (who can try cases if the litigants assent) and bankruptcy judges. (Bankruptcy court will be largely autonomous from the district court in 1984.) Law clerks to the judges will sometimes answer questions.

In 1980, about 3500 civil cases were filed at the court, some of them involving the government, some involving only private parties. In addition, nearly 650 criminal cases and over 400 bankruptcy cases began that year. Reporters and researchers can find the case files in the clerk's office on the first floor. Anyone may inspect the files and pay for photocopies. The cases are indexed; microfilm and computerized printouts of litigants' names, case numbers and names of presiding judges are available. To keep up with new filings, it is wise to examine each month's cover sheets. These are forms listing the litigants, the type of case, a brief explanation of the complaint, the presiding judge and the lawyers for each side. In a separate room on the first floor, daily schedules for each judge are posted.

One way to keep current without visiting the court each day is to subscribe to a legal daily. Almost every major city has one: Washington is no exception. *The Daily Washington Law Reporter* reports decisions as well as listing new cases filed. Telephone inquiries to the court about the status of a case are possible if the investigator knows the case number or the name of the presiding judge. A call to the clerk's office or the judge's chamber will often elicit the desired information. There is a press room on the fourth floor of the courthouse. A handful of reporters have cubicles there. Telephones, bathrooms and sofas are available.

The U.S. Tax Court, located on the edge of Capitol Hill, hears disputes between the Internal Revenue Service and tax-payers—that is, if the disputed tax is being withheld. (If a tax-payer wants to pay first, then fight, he goes to another court for the refund.) The authorized size of the court is nineteen judges, appointed by the president for fifteen-year terms. The chief judgeship rotates. The court has the authority to name ten special trial judges, who listen to disputes involving less than $5000. One judge is assigned to a case; many hearings are held outside Washington. At the start of 1981, about 35,000 cases were pending. Investigators will find cases filed according to taxpayer name and by state. Someone interested in cases from a particular geographic area, therefore, does not have to search through every file drawer. If the investigator wants to learn whether a particular person is embroiled in a tax dispute, the alphabetical name file works well.

Bill Ringle of the Gannett Washington Bureau has written many stories inspired by tax court documents. One involved ap-parent Mafia infiltration of a dress company in a small city near one of Gannett's dailies. Ringle was tipped off to the Mafia tie by recognizing the name of a dress company executive in what otherwise appeared to be a routine case involving a small amount of disputed tax.

The Court of Claims, located near the White House, hears three main types of cases: requests for back pay from civilian or military employees, suits from government contractors, and tax cases if the the plaintiff has already paid the IRS. The federal government is always the defendant in this court. Suits can involve other issues, too, including unauthorized use by the government of a patented invention, payment for land taken by the government, or Indian claims. The amounts at stake are often sizable, the facts often compelling by any standard. Yet most Washington correspondents ignore the court.

O'Shea, who prided himself on digging stories out of court files while a correspondent for the *Des Moines Register*, said, "I don't think most reporters even know where the Court of Claims is located." The *Washington Star's* Denniston, author of the book *The Reporter and the Law*, noted that the cases contain "some very fascinating factual issues, and, now and then, legal questions. At most, however, it provides the basis for intermittent feature stories. . .about given cases of notable novelty."

An investigator checking files in December 1980 would have found a case questioning whether a government employee could be fired because of allegations he had molested a young girl. A reporter covering California would have found interesting a court award of $1.5 million, plus twelve years interest, to Georgia-Pacific, a corporation which had sued the government over payment for 3368 acres taken to establish Redwood National Park.

Another duty of the court is to help Congress act intelligently on private bills—those introduced for the benefit of individual persons or entities. Court personnel become involved with private bills only at the request of Congress.

Trials are conducted throughout the United States, and sometimes in foreign countries. Normally, one of the sixteen court-appointed trial judges hears the case first. The trial judge recommends a decision; it is almost always contested. If that happens, the case goes to a panel of three judges or to the entire court—seven judges, including the chief judge. They are appointed by the president and serve for life. The court reads briefs filed by aggrieved parties and hears oral arguments. Parties can go directly to the Supreme Court after a claims court ruling.

Decisions are eventually published by the Government Printing Office in *United States Court of Claims Reports*. They are available almost immediately, however, in the clerk of the court's office. Trial judge rulings are not officially published, but are also available through the clerk. An investigator wanting to learn whether an individual or business has sued the government in the court can look in the alphabetical card file found in the clerk's office. Someone interested in the estate of Howard Hughes would find a listing there. Or a reporter in the Washington bureau of the *St. Louis Post-Dispatch* would find a file card for McDonnell Douglas, a corporation headquartered in St. Louis.

The Court of Customs and Patent Appeals, located in the same building as the Court of Claims, hears appeals from rulings of the Court of International Trade, based in New York City. It also hears appeals from the U.S. Patent and Trademark Office (part of the Commerce Department), from certain U.S. International Trade Commission decisions, and from some rulings by the secretary of commerce and secretary of agriculture. The five judges, including the chief judge, are nominated by the president for life and confirmed by the Senate. They usually hear cases in Washington, D.C., but sometimes sit elsewhere. Aggrieved parties can go directly to the Supreme Court after a ruling from this court. Investigators interested in determining whether someone is involved in a case can use the alphabetical card file in the clerk's office. The file is cross-referenced according to plaintiff and defendant. In 1981, Fred Barbash of the *Washington Post* wrote about a dispute between the court and the Justice Department over whether patent applications based on computer programs should be granted. Barbash reported that resolution of the dispute by the Supreme Court might affect 3000 patent applications potentially worth billions of dollars.

In 1980, Congress came close to approving consolidation of the Court of Claims and the Court of Customs and Patent Appeals into a newly created U.S. Court of Appeals for the Federal Circuit. The legislation also would have established a claims court to assume the trial duties of the current Court of Claims. Such a bill might become law in the 97th Congress during 1981-82.

The Court of Military Appeals, at the edge of Capitol Hill, consists of a chief judge and two other judges, appointed by the president to fifteen-year terms. The judges are civilians. It is an appellate court only; there is no further review from its decisions by a higher court. Each military service has its own court of review below this tribunal to hear appeals from special or general court-martial proceedings. Rarely is this court covered by Washington correspondents.

An exception was the 1973 hearing for William Calley, who was charged with mass murder in Vietnam. The parties filed briefs and argued their cases before the judges. The court eventually confirmed Calley's conviction. Another exception was described in a 1980 article by Jonathan Poses, Washington correspondant for *Enlisted Times*. Poses reported on the controversy about whether Judge Robinson Everett—just confirmed by the Senate—would swing the progressive court back in a conservative direction more to the liking of the Defense Department.

In addition to the courts already mentioned, there are certain federal "courts" convened in special circumstances. These courts are composed of district and appellate judges who sit on them in addition to the courts to which they are appointed:

• The Temporary Emergency Court of Appeals consists of panels of three judges who hear energy-related cases. The jurisdiction is limited to cases under three laws: the Emergency Petroleum Allocation Act, Emergency Natural Gas Act and Energy Policy and Conservation Act. In 1979-80, about ninety cases were filed. One 1980 ruling said oil refiners could raise gasoline prices to recover as much as $17 billion for income lost due to improperly fixed federal price ceilings. Despite the importance of energy cases, few Washington correspondents have heard of the court, much less covered it. Even reporters at the top energy newsletter in Washington said they generally are unaware of the deci-

sions. One exception was the *Legal Times of Washington.*
Managing editor Diana Huffman said her reporters pick up
decisions regularly because of the significant energy matters
involved.

• The U.S. Foreign Intelligence Surveillance Court considers
requests from the Justice Department for electronic
surveillance in cases involving foreign matters. There is also
a review court that considers denials of surveillance
applications.

• The Rail Reorganization Court was established to determine the value of properties transferred by large bankrupt
railroads in the Northeast and Midwest.

The investigator who need statistics or other information
about federal courts can do one-stop shopping at the Administrative Office of the U.S. Courts; this office has data on the
15,000-person federal judiciary. The office prepares the
judicial branch budget submitted to Congress. Its annual report
on the workload of the federal judiciary contains a wealth of
useful, detailed information. Specific reports are sometimes
useful, too—for example, by law the office must provide Congress with an annual accounting of wiretaps authorized by
federal and state judges.

Another entity, the Federal Judicial Center, publishes
research on improving the judicial system. In the basement of
its building is a library that is open to the public and that contains a great deal of practical information, centralized so an investigator need not traverse the city in search of what he is
looking for.

The policy making arm of the judiciary is the Judicial Conference of the United States, presided over by the chief justice
of the the Supreme Court. It usually meets twice a year, and its
decisions can have far-reaching effects. For example, in 1980
the *New York Times* reported a Judicial Conference recommen-
dation adopted by the Supreme Court. Because of the new rule,
journalists and other investigators have limited access to
documents in court cases that routinely had been part of the
public record. The documents include affidavits, depositions

and other materials produced in the pretrial fact-finding process called "discovery." Rule changes recommended by the Judicial Conference and approved by the Supreme Court take effect unless disapproved by Congress within a specified period.

The next chapter moves away from government institutions to look at special interests in the private sector. The Washington-based special interests, as well as lobbyists for special interests located outside the area, have a tremendous impact on the federal government.

'I REPEAT—THERE IS NO REAL CAUSE FOR ALARM...'

The Special Interests in the Private Sector

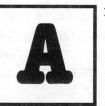

n investigator in Washington, D.C. is failing to do his job well if he develops sources and tracks issues only in the legislative, executive and judicial branches. On every issue, forces outside the government are at work. They provide information—sometimes supplemented by money and other political weapons—in an attempt to get their way. These diverse non-governmental forces can be grouped under the title "special interests."

Some special interests in Washington go it alone. At least several hundred individual business corporations are represented by a new breed called "vice president for government relations" or something similar. Numerous labor unions, states, counties, cities, universities and professions also staff their own Washington offices. In addition, special interests are frequently represented in the capital by a trade association; an oil company with its own lobbyists here also might belong to the

American Petroleum Institute. In early 1981, a generally accepted count of associations headquartered in Washington was 2500. These associations employed an estimated 100,000 people in the capital and had combined budgets of about $5 billion.

But that is only the beginning. Other special interests include the multi-issue, political-ideological groups (the liberal Americans for Democratic Action or the American Conservative Union); people from diverse occupations joining together to accomplish one goal (a cleaner environment or handgun control); people joining together to influence government policy because of their age, gender, skin color or ethnicity (the American Association of Retired Persons, National Organization for Women, National Association for the Advancement of Colored People and Polish American Congress); "think tanks" with an intellectual stake in seeing their policies adopted; foundations that distribute money; and private consulting firms located throughout the urban area. Furthermore, there are law firms, public relation firms and others that represent clients seeking to influence the government.

"These special pleaders can be extremely helpful to journalists," comments Edmund Lambeth, a long-time Washington correspondent who now teaches journalism at Indiana University. "So many reporters ignore them because they think that their bias precludes useful contact. But that's not true."

Art Wiese, Washington Bureau chief for the *Houston Post*, says the "public relations staffs of the trade associations and corporations have to be mentioned. These people are often very good sources."

Getting a Handle on the Special Interests

An investigator will be on as many mailing lists as possible if he wants to keep track of the public activities of the special interests. But news releases are only a beginning. The effective investigator must understand that no controversy can be fully comprehended through government sources alone. He knows to seek out special interests, even if he thinks of them pejoratively as "lobbyists." (Most lobbyists are, in fact, honest men and women who have access to useful information. Like journalists, their main asset is credibility. For that reason, they rarely provide false information intentionally.)

But how to find the best source in the vast realm of private interests? One way is to ask sources inside the government. A Senate or House committee staffer handling an issue might be willing to tell an investigator the identities of lobbyists buzzing around the committee room. Directories are often preferable, however, to haphazard reliance on human sources. The telephone book shows whether a particular business, university or other institution has a Washington representative. In the yellow pages under the heading "associations," there are hundreds of listings. Another printed source is the *Washington Information Directory* published by Congressional Quarterly. The 1980-81 edition contains nearly 1000 pages divided into sixteen main topics such as "energy" and "national security." Each chapter is subdivided, so subjects such as coal, nuclear and petroleum are found under the heading "energy." Within each subdivision are key government agencies, congressional committees and non-governmental groups that deal with the topic daily.

Other frequently used directories include *Who's Who in Association Management*, published by the Washington-based American Society of Association Executives, the "association for associations"; *National Trade and Professional Associations of the United States and Canada and Labor Unions* published by Columbia Books in Washington, D.C.; the *Encyclopedia of Associations* published by Gale Research Co. in Detroit; *Public Interest Profiles*, a guide to 100 leading so-called public interest groups in Washington, D.C., available from the local Foundation for Public Affairs; *O'Dwyer's Directory of Public Relations Firms* by the J.R. O'Dwyer Co., New York City; *Washington Lobbyists/Lawyers Directory* published by Washington-based Am Ward Publications; and the *Martindale-Hubbell Law Directory* from Martindale-Hubbell in Summit, N.J. The American League of Lobbyists membership list might be of use, too; its several hundred members work mostly for national corporations. The Business-Government Relations Council publishes a directory of members, who are the senior legislative liaison/lobbyists for national businesses and industrial organizations.

These and other umbrella directories (used in conjunction with public documents about individual lobbyists) help investigators keep tabs on those who usually would rather stay out of the public eye.

What public documents? Under the 1946 Regulation of Lobbying Act, certain lobbyists must register with and then regularly report to the clerk of the House and the secretary of the Senate. New registrations and financial reports from previous registrants are compiled each quarter and published in the *Congressional Record*. (Registrations from the third quarter of 1980 were published in the *Record* November 21, so there is a lag.) Another source is *Congressional Quarterly Weekly Report*; it publishes registrations regularly.

There are loopholes in the law, though, created in part by poor drafting and in part by a 1954 Supreme Court decision validating the law's constitutionality. Some people considered to be lobbyists by themselves and everyone else are exempted from filing reports because they spend only their own money: The Supreme Court ruled that the law covers only groups soliciting or collecting money to influence legislation. The court also said the law allows Washington representatives to determine what proportion of their total expenditures is allocated to lobbying. Thus, a lobbyist can allege money was spent for "public education," when actually it was spent on attempts to influence legislation. Furthermore, the Court held that the law applies only to groups whose principal purpose is influencing legislation through direct contacts with congressmen. If a group does other things besides lobbying, if certain congressional staffers (rather than elected congressmen) are the targets, or if the lobbying is done by letters from group members outside Washington, the group may not have to file reports. According to Norman J. Ornstein and Shirley Elder in their book *Interest Groups, Lobbying and Policymaking*, another loophole is that the law fails to cover attempts to influence executive branch decision making.

Attempts to reform the law have been the subject of numerous stories. One, which appeared in *Business Week* during 1980, noted changes opposed by private groups that rarely agree on anything: "With the exception of Common Cause and the AFL-CIO, nearly everyone who buttonholes members of Congress or prepares position papers objects to tough lobby reform."

With so many loopholes to worry about, why should an investigator even bother to consult public records in the House and Senate? Because, however incomplete, the records reflect which groups care about which issues. A look through just one month's registrations turned up fifty-nine businesses, forty-nine trade associations, four labor groups, four state and local governments, ten citizens groups and others. The University of Texas system registered as a lobbyist on the crude oil windfall profits tax bill. A group calling itself the Federation for American Immigration Reform said it was planning to influence the number and kinds of foreigners allowed into the United States. Brown & Williamson Tobacco Corp. reported it was working on legislation concerning the Federal Trade Commission, an agency known for occasionally tough action against cigarette companies and advertising claims.

Perhaps even more obscure than the 1946 lobbying law is the Foreign Agents Registration Act of 1938—although thanks to the case involving the Libyan government and Billy Carter in 1980, the law was briefly in the limelight. Deaver and Hannaford, a public relations firm with links to Ronald Reagan, also inadvertently publicized the law in the *Washington Post* news columns during 1980. The publicity occurred after questions were raised about the legality of the firm failing to register while working for Guatemalan businessmen hoping to erase their country's image as a human rights violator. Michael Deaver, a partner in the firm, later was appointed deputy chief of staff in the Reagan White House. As a result of the story, investigators began to appreciate the availability of the information on file at the Justice Department. In fact, the *Washington Star* ran a front-page story detailing all fifty-four legal actions brought by the Justice Department from 1938 to 1980.

Foreign agents must file not only regular reports but also copies of political propaganda disseminated in America. The Justice Department publishes a monthly news release of registrations. By examining the files, *New York Times* reporter Clyde Farnsworth determined that Japan had more foreign agents registered in the United States as of 1980 than any other country. Farnsworth wrote that during the early 1970s the Japanese were surprised when the U.S. government imposed an import surcharge and disrupted a Japanese economy heavily dependent on exports to America. But with about 100 groups or individuals registered as Washington representatives for Japanese interests, the *Times* story said Japan was no longer likely to be caught unaware.

An interesting note: A study by *Congressional Quarterly Weekly Report* revealed that at least eighteen former members of Congress, a former Central Intelligence Agency director and a former secretary of defense had registered as foreign agents.

The Special Interests—What They Do and How They Do It

Private groups initiate or oppose legislation and regulations to further their own interests. Having competent draftsmen and strategists in the organization helps. But just as important is access to congressmen who are in accord with a group's beliefs, or who might be converted. If a congressman can be convinced the tax code should provide greater incentives for building new factories, he will then order his personal or committee staff to draft the appropriate language. The desire for access is part of the reason why special interest groups employ former members of Congress. Former congressmen retain their right to be on the floor of the chamber. Ex-members can eat in the legislators' private dining room or use the gymnasium; these are privileges denied other lobbyists. Also, ex-members often receive priority treatment if they want to testify before a congressional committee.

During 1980, *Congressional Quarterly Weekly Report* ran an article stating at least sixty former congressmen were working as lobbyists in Washington. Former Colorado Representative Donald Brotzman had joined the Rubber Manufacturers Association; Mike McKevitt, another former House member from Colorado, had turned to lobbying for the National Federation of Independent Business; former U.S. Senator Robert Taft Jr. was representing the Grocery Manufacturers of America, the American Hospital Association and other organizations.

Special interests employ the same approach in lobbying the executive branch—retain somebody who has been there. It was no coincidence that Ford Motor Co. retained former secretary of transportation William Coleman when the automaker was facing a massive recall ordered by the Department of Transportation. Nor was it coincidence that Roderick Hills, former Securities and Exchange Commission chairman, was retained by companies regulated by the SEC.

Not all effective lobbyists are former congressmen or Cabinet secretaries. Many are lawyers—anonymous to nearly everybody but the members of Congress, congressional staffers, presidential appointees and career bureaucrats on whom they work their magic. Some of these lawyers have served in government, some have not. In late 1980, the *Washington Star's* Pat Lewis profiled lawyer J.D. Williams, naming him one of the truly powerful lobbyists, whose clients ranged from Pillsbury to E.F. Hutton. Williams had never held an important federal post—his clout came from other connections. Then age forty-three, he headed a seventeen-member law firm. Lewis said she knew little about Williams before beginning the profile, but learned that "he is considered to be one of the biggies." Having never seen a lobbyist in action, Lewis was surprised "at how much money was involved. I wish I had more time to look into what his clients pay him."

The name of Williams' firm, Williams and Jensen, was not on the tip of everyone's tongue. But a few Washington law firms are so prestigious that their names evoke widespread recognition: Covington and Burling, Hogan and Hartson, Arnold and Porter, among others. In 1980, those were probably the three largest Washington-based firms. (Covington and Burling employed about 200 attorneys.) Not surprisingly, they received business from special interest groups.

Hundreds of law firms are specialized, but well-known in their particular fields. When *Broadcasting* magazine ran a report about communications lawyers during 1980, it noted dozens of firms that exercised clout in Washington on behalf of television, radio, cable and telephone clients. The most frequently named lawyer-lobbyists in the field often had experience on Capitol Hill or at the Federal Communications Commission. The *Broadcasting* article was especially valuable because it listed clients of Washington law firms. The client lists were compiled in part by combing through filings by the law firms at regulatory agencies and in the courts.

The number of law firms that have Washington offices but are based in other cities is growing; they are challenging Washington-based firms for business. A 1980 survey by *Legal Times of Washington*, a weekly newspaper, found 179 branch offices of out-of-town law firms. New York was home base to about one-third of the branch offices. Los Angeles and Chicago also were well-represented. When Walter Mondale stepped down as vice president of the United States in 1981, he joined the Washington office of a Chicago firm. The *Washington Post, Washington Star* and *Wall Street Journal* all ran stories on the Washington branch office phenomenon, using the *Legal Times* survey for background.

Former, congressmen, one-time executive branch officials and lawyer-lobbyists share their business with another breed—the public relations specialists. Some of the public relations firms have large numbers of well-connected people working for them in Washington. In early 1981, the Hill and Knowlton office had a staff of eighty, many of them former congressional staffers. In fact, Robert Gray chaired President Reagan's inauguration committee while at the same time heading Hill and Knowlton's Washington office. The Reagan administration reached into Hill and Knowlton's office for several important appointees, including Nancy Reagan's press secretary, Sheila Patton. Other public relations clients are business corporations and trade associations. U.S. government agencies, foreign interests, charities and so-called public interest groups also hire Washington public relations-lobbyists.

Evaluating the effectiveness of public relations firms is difficult, just as it is difficult to evaluate the true effectiveness of lawyer-lobbyists. But when listening to the public relations lobbyists talk, it is easy to conclude that they often affect government policy.

Hill and Knowlton executives told *National Journal* reporter Michael Gordon in 1980 that they helped turn the tide against a Food and Drug Administration proposal to ban saccharin. Hill and Knowlton's client was the Calorie Control Council, an organization dominated by the soft drink industry. Executives at Burson-Marsteller, another large public relations firm, told Gordon they played a role in submarining a Federal Trade Commission inquiry into television advertising aimed at children.

Gordon said he wrote his in-depth story on public relations firms in Washington because "I wondered about the scope of their operations and their influence. A lot of clients pay a lot of money for their services. . .The big effort by Hill and Knowlton on behalf of trucking deregulation really intrigued me. I knew enough to be able to tell what was factual and what wasn't."

By developing sources in the private sector, an investigator can discover more than merely who is lobbying whom about what. He can obtain information difficult to find elsewhere. At times, the federal government itself relies on private industry data in order to make policy. The Energy Department reportedly was relying on figures from the American Petroleum Institute about oil reserves, and the Department of Health and Human Services allegedly was dependent on the American Hospital Association for data about hospital care costs.

An investigator can unearth useful information by reading newsletters and other publications published by special interests. The most informative publications are often those intended for members only, though special-interest publications intended for a wider audience can be useful, too. An investigator following the debate over revenue sharing would find few more informed, timely sources than *County News,* a weekly published by the National Association of Counties. Independent newsletters and magazines that specialize in a narrow topic can be treasure troves of information as well, because they cover what private interests are doing. In 1981 the *Washingtonian* magazine ran an article describing many of the most respected, influential specialized publications in the nation's capital.

To gain an overview of important issues in a field, an investigator should look for booklets like the one issued twice a year by the National Association of Broadcasters. The January 1980 edition, titled *Broadcasting and Government: A Review of 1979 and a Preview of 1980,* ran seventy-four pages. In that space, it covered about 100 controversies of interest to the NAB. The booklet—like others available from various special interests—is generally understandable and costs nothing.

Many special interest groups publish lists of experts inside the organizations; a pamphlet from the Chamber of Commerce of the United States naming its staff specialists is an example. Special-interest liaisons to Congress and the agencies almost always know the status of a proposed bill or regulation. Spokesmen for some private groups become so well-known that journalists call them automatically—Art Pine wrote in the *Washington Post* that among the mavens of the media are Michael Sumichrast of the National Association of Home Builders and John Lichtblau of the Petroleum Industry Research Foundation.

A public interest group is like a trade association, but its goal is often not economic gain. As one public interest group veteran says, "We are nothing but a special interest group with no money." The publications and staffs of these groups provide a valuable counterpoint. For every National Association of Broadcasters, there is a National Citizens Committee for Broadcasting. For every association of defense contractors, there is a Center for Defense Information. The groups testify before Congress, comment on executive branch proceedings, and generally do what the corporations, local governments and trade associations represented in Washington do. Sometimes they, too, employ former government insiders. In 1981, recently defeated U.S. Senator Gaylord Nelson of Wisconsin and Representative Joseph Fisher of Virginia, considered to be environmental supporters in Congress, were hired by the Wilderness Society.

Private, not-for-profit "think tanks" in Washington are not exactly special interest groups in the same sense as the Chamber of Commerce or AFL-CIO, nor are they precisely akin to public interest groups. Rarely do they actively lobby Congress or the agencies. Instead, they churn out studies and books and let their research do the talking. Probably the best-known of the organizations are the Brookings Institution and the American Enterprise Institute for Public Policy Research. Both had 1980 budgets of close to $11 million. Brookings had fifty resident scholars; AEI had thirty-four. Brookings is generally labeled as Democratic and left-of-center; AEI as Republican and right-of-center. During the first month of his administration, Ronald Reagan named seventeen persons from AEI to significant positions. Even if the experts at Brookings and AEI have biases, they are viewed as experts nonetheless. Brookings, AEI and the avowedly liberal Institute for Policy Studies do most of their own research, usually remaining financially and philosophically beholden to no one. The books and pamphlets turned out by resident and visiting scholars range over hundreds of topics. In 1980 AEI put out 125 new publications and four periodicals; Brookings published twenty books. Catalogs listing available publications are distributed by all three organizations. Seminars and conferences are often based on the topic of a forthcoming or just-released study.

Other influential—but little-known—think tanks (for example, the Urban Institute, Rand Corporation and SRI International) produce numerous reports under government contract.

According to a 1980 *Omni* magazine profile, perhaps the most prestigious military think tank is the Institute for Defense Analyses. Author Paul Nahin, a former staffer there, said almost all of the $30 million budget was provided by the Pentagon. Despite the taxpayer money involved, Nahin said he was unable to obtain a list of even the unclassified publications published by the Institute.

When a government-sponsored report is unavailable from a think tank, it might be obtained from the government itself. Technical and scientific documents produced for the government are available through the National Technical Information Service (part of the Commerce Department). The documents are indexed and abstracted in *Government Reports Announcements and Index*, which appears every other week. Nontechnical documents of general interest appear in catalogs from the Government Printing Office.

Whether or not the think tanks are primarily government-funded, their thinkers tend to commute between government jobs and the not-for-profit corridors. At the Center for Strategic and International Studies (affiliated with Georgetown University), the chairman in 1980—David Abshire—had served in a high-ranking State Department job. He also had been helping the administration of Ronald Reagan take over from the Carter administration. This swinging door effect often makes sources at think tanks more valuable: They have not only written about the making of public policy, but also have shaped it themselves.

Daniel Schorr, veteran Washington television reporter and author of *Clearing the Air*, tells of how he was led to CSIS after being assigned by CBS to investigate Central Intelligence Agency involvement in the overthrow of Chilean President Salvador Allende. At the think tank, Schorr found Ray Cline, a former high-ranking CIA official and the first knowledgeable source who would agree to talk about the matter on camera.

Many think tanks receive funding from foundations, and in fact most foundations in Washington exist primarily to disperse money to outside organizations. But some organizations with the word "foundation" in their title actually conduct their own research and publish the results. The Heritage Foundation's much-heralded 3000-page transition study for President Reagan is an example.

Think tanks and other private interests sometimes try to influence opinion by holding annual conventions or seminars in Washington. For investigators, the attraction is that hundreds of knowledgeable sources are gathered in one place, brains ripe for picking, mouths ripe for gossiping. Speakers frequently include congressmen and bureaucrats who reveal new policies to the intensely interested audience. Not so incidentally, the policy maker may be paid a hefty honorarium that might help him look upon the special interest favorably the next time it approaches him for help.

Playing Political Hardball

News releases, research reports and seminars might occasionally influence public policy. But vote ratings and political contributions are what many private interests use when they are serious about getting attention. At least fifty organizations publish vote ratings of congressmen. The Democratic Congressional Campaign Committee (an adjunct of Democratic House members) publishes a compilation of group ratings each year. Ratings come from groups as diverse as the Chamber of Commerce, the AFL-CIO and Ralph Nader's Public Citizen.

Ratings must be used with care. They do nothing more than record how a congressman voted on a handful of issues considered important by one special interest group. The floor votes are a biased sample of all votes in Congress every year. The ratings almost always fail to account for a congressman's committee activity. Usually, the ratings cannot even be used to say that a congressman is "pro" or "anti" something. For example, in agriculture, two powerful lobbies—the National Farmers Union and The American Farm Bureau Federation—may give diametrically opposed rankings to the same congressman. The two organizations have different beliefs and select different floor votes to evaluate whether a member of Congress has endorsed those beliefs.

Despite their flaws, vote ratings are frequently used by political action committees in determining which congressmen to support monetarily. Many major corporations, trade associations and labor unions have political action committees. So do an increasing number of ideological or religious groups unconnected to any business or union.

At the beginning of 1981, the Federal Election Commission counted 1204 political action committees sponsored by corporations, 574 affiliated with trade and other membership groups, 297 connected to labor unions and 378 non-connected PACs. The committees allocate money using their own criteria.

Studying requests for advisory opinions at the Federal Election Commission may provide clues to new wrinkles in a PAC's operation. At least a few PACs publish information (intended for members) about how they raise and spend money. Often, the Washington representative of the sponsoring organization plays a key role in deciding who will receive money.

During the 1980 campaigns, the Associated General Contractors of America said it would use 10 percent of its money for Washington fundraising events organized on behalf of congressional candidates. Of the remaining 90 percent, most went to incumbents in close races, or to incumbents needing financial assistance who voted in accord with the contractors' positions. Occasionally, money was given to a challenger if the incumbent's voting record was objectionable. But challengers were unlikely to receive money—no matter how objectionable the incumbent—if the incumbent had won his last race with more than 75 percent of the vote. PAC contributions to candidates for president are sometimes mentioned to the victor later on when the sponsoring organization tries to influence selection of appointees for key executive branch jobs.

The political action committees must register with the Federal Election Commission. Registration is required by law within ten days after a PAC is formed. During an election year, a PAC can file monthly or quarterly. Those filing quarterly, however, must file special reports for primary elections. In non-election years, reports are due less frequently. Contributions from individuals to the PAC must be itemized if they total $200 in a calendar year. Common Cause, among others, has issued studies indicating links between PAC contributions and the way members of Congress vote. But it is hard to tell sometimes whether a congressman voted a certain way because he had been given money, or whether the money was given because the congressman had voted correctly in the past.

The Social Scene: Private Parties and Public Policy

Many observers believe that much of Washington's business begins after hours at private parties given by special interests. Ron Nessen, a former NBC Washington correspondent and press secretary to President Ford, wrote in *TV Guide* that the *Washington Post* Style section may provide a more accurate picture of what is happening in Washington than the news columns do. The parties covered in the *Post* and in the *Washington Star's* Washington Life section are where the real work of the city often is done, Nessen said.

The Washington social scene is an extension of the work day, a time when policy makers and influence peddlers have additional access to one another. The main entertainment at a Washington party is talk, not music or dancing. According to a 1980 *Washington Journalism Review* article by Susan Watters, journalists are more desirable guests at social events than ever before. Some Washington correspondents and columnists refuse to mingle with sources or potential sources at parties. Other journalists say they attend parties willingly and consider the evening a bust if they do not learn something new.

The parties usually receiving the most attention are White House functions. Not a great deal of business is conducted at these events, but they seem important nonetheless. The *Post* and the *Star* often publish guest lists, so everybody can see who is "in" and who is "out." In a city where perceptions of who has the president's ear matter, having one's own name on the list is significant. The establishment guide of who is in and who is out is the Green Book, so named because of its green velvet cover.

The *New York Times* noted in a 1981 article that the Green
Book hoped to offer subscribers a special supplement so that
hosts would know whom from the Reagan administration to in-
vite to parties. Officially called the *Social List of Washington
D.C.*, the book is published privately by Jean Shaw Murray,
whose grandmother founded it in 1930. Decisions about whom
to include are made by a board of governors; most suggestions
for additions come from persons already listed, Murray said.

Unlike the social registers in most cities, persons named in
the Green Book are as likely to be there because of official position or perceived political power as they are because of family
pedigree. The book provides otherwise hard-to-obtain home
telephone numbers and addresses for many of the personages
included.

Parties staged by trade associations or other special interests at such places as hotels or private clubs may be important forums for making contacts. The guests tend to be congressmen and their aides, bureaucrats and others in a position
to help or harm the special interest. Parties in the homes of
lawyers, public relations practitioners and other lobbyists are
more subtle in purpose, but people on the guest list are usually
included by design. There is always the talk about after-dinner
poker games where the lobbyists suddenly become lousy card
players and the congressman-guest ends up with big winnings.

Foreign embassies' parties are frequently given and more
public. Adlai Stevenson, himself an experienced diplomat, once
said that an ambassador's job "is composed of equal parts of
alcohol, protocol and Geritol." The constant social obligations
may become a bore, but embassy functions—like other
Washington parties—are an extension of work where intelligence and rumor can be gathered.

A conversation at an Austrian party in mid-1980 apparently led Benjamin Civiletti, who was then attorney general, to
make the surprise disclosure that he had spoken earlier with
President Carter about the problems of Carter's brother Billy.
Civiletti had previously denied discussing the matter with the
president. But at the ambassador's party, presidential

counselor Lloyd Cutler saw Civiletti, according to an account by Zofia Smardz in the *Washington Star*, and took the attorney general aside to remind him of his earlier exchange with the president. According to newspaper accounts, Civiletti and Cutler were only two of the highpowered guests at the Austrian ambassador's. Others included the secretary of energy, secretary of the Navy, deputy secretary of defense, head of the Office of Management and Budget, three senators, a House member and a Supreme Court justice.

Not only ambassadors, but also private foreign interests, are known for their parties. South Korean wheeler-dealer Tongsun Park opened his George Town Club in the 1960s. For years he threw parties there as part of his high-stakes, multimillion dollar strategy to buy influence for Korea in Congress. It was much later that journalists and government officials became aware of Park's wrongdoing eventually leading to his indictment—although some investigators say they had suspicions from the start. Maxine Cheshire of the *Washington Post*, author of *Maxine Cheshire: Reporter*, kept her eye on Park from the day his club opened. Cheshire said as Park's parties grew more lavish and his houses grew larger and larger, "I could not help feeling that there was something amiss, for Tongsun Park was not a man of wealth."

To keep tabs on the official foreign community, an investigator can acquire directories from the Government Printing Office. They include the *Diplomatic List, Employees of Diplomatic Missions* and *Foreign Consular Offices in the United States*. Many embassies have press and political officers who can be helpful in providing information and explanations.

One type of special interest has been omitted from this chapter—the political party. The Democratic and Republican organizations in Washington, D.C., within Congress and outside it, can yield a great deal of information for the investigator. The major parties are the subject of the next chapter.

The Political Parties

Only a handful of Washington reporters cover what Jack Germond of the *Washington Star* calls "the political industry"—the Republican and Democratic parties, affiliated organizations and campaign consultants. The coverage increases slightly every two years during congressional campaigns, and significantly every four years because of the race for the Presidency.

The vast majority of Washington correspondents who ignore the parties as sources of information—especially during odd-numbered years—are making a mistake. Stories emanating from Congress, the White House and elsewhere in Washington can often be enhanced by using sources at the party organizations within Congress, including the four congressional campaign committees; at the Republican and Democratic National committees; and within the ranks of the political consultants.

The Parties Inside Congress

"Congress Chiefs Predict Big Changes in Tax Plan," said a *New York Times* headline in early 1981. *Times* reporter Steven Roberts, who wrote the story under the headline, quoted sources as saying that President Reagan's tax proposals would be "substantially altered before they are passed into law." Who did Roberts talk to for the story? House Speaker Thomas O'Neill Jr. and House Majority Leader Jim Wright, among others. O'Neill and Wright were the top leaders of the House Democrats in the 97th Congress. The Republicans in the House have their leaders, too, as do the Democrats and Republicans in the Senate. These leaders, and the mini-bureaucracies that serve them, can be valuable sources to investigators.

In 1981, Senate Majority Leader Howard Baker Jr. held Thursday morning briefings. John Tower, a Texas senator who chaired the Senate Republican Policy Committee, met with reporters every Tuesday after Policy Committee lunches. The Policy Committee publishes numerous reports of potential use to investigators, including a "Legislative Notice" for each bill sent to the Senate floor, a "Record Vote Analysis" of every recorded vote taking place in the Senate, personal voting records of senators published as "the Bobtail," policy papers on major issues and much more.

Senate Democrats were led by Robert Byrd of West Virginia as of 1981. His Saturday morning news conferences usually made Sunday headlines. The Senate Democratic Policy Committee, under Byrd's direction, publishes the "Democratic Legislative Bulletin," summarizing bills on the calendar and listing possible amendments.

"I went to virtually every one of Senator Byrd's Saturday briefings, and wrote a story about what he said, whether it was big news or not," said Robert Furlow, who covered the Senate for the Associated Press in 1980. Furlow said the wire services generally staff the Baker and Tower briefings, too.

Furlow added that he occasionally used Senate leadership publications for background. "But those kinds of things are much easier to find in the House," he said. "If I were covering a bill that I didn't know much about, I would grab a background bulletin and educate myself."

House party leadership organizations are, as Furlow suggests, more prolific than their Senate counterparts in publishing information of use to investigators. Rank-and-file House Democrats and Republicans, apart from the leadership, have formed groups that churn out publications with regularity.

The House Republican Conference publishes a weekly "Legislative Digest" which provides handy summaries of every bill that is expected to be considered by the House during the next five days. The summaries include the adminstration's position, projected costs and views of dissenting congressmen. A daily supplement lists amendments expected to be offered on the House floor. In 1980, the Republican Conference also published a briefing book, "Issues '80," with details on matters expected to be debated by the Congress.

The House Republican Research Committee and House Republican Policy Committee, additional arms of the leadership, provide material on both specific legislation and long-term issues. The research committee formed nine task forces in 1981 to study issues and put their findings into "white papers." The policy committee suggests to House Republicans how they might want to vote on legislation. Its thirty-three members meet weekly, and usually issue a news release about the policy decisions that were reached.

Among non-leadership groups on the Republican side of the House, the Republican Study Committee is the most prolific. About 150 members of Congress pay to belong; their contributions financed a fourteen-member staff in 1981. "Fact Sheets" on individual bills, Supreme Court decisions and major issues; a "Legislative Preview" keyed to the following week's House schedule; and other regular and occasional publications of the committee can provide investigators with views generally more conservative than those of the House Republican leadership.

A Republican non-leadership organization that considers itself more moderate-to-liberal than the Study Committee is the

House Wednesday Group. Members must be invited to join—in 1981 there were thirty-two representatives and fourteen senators, plus a small staff. Its background papers are lengthy and specific. Examples from 1980 included a twenty-four-page background report on U.S. immigration and refugee policy and an eighteen-page report on U.S. military manpower. The name of the staffer who prepared the paper is provided on the last page.

The Democratic leadership in the House is available to journalists on a regular basis. As of 1981, Speaker O'Neill held a briefing fifteen minutes before the House convened each day it was in session. Majority Whip Thomas Foley, a Washington State congressman, held Friday morning briefings. Foley's office issued a "Whip Advisory" whenever a bill was about to go to the floor for debate. An investigator interested in internal congressional reform can seek out the chairman of the House Democratic Caucus, to which all Democratic representatives belong. Richard Lyons of the *Washington Post* reported that the caucus' 1981 chairman, Representative Gillis Long of Louisiana, "thinks the caucus should stay away from legislation for fear it would lead to pressuring members into supporting positions they oppose. He thinks the caucus should focus on refining some of the procedural changes of the past decade, such as shrinking the proliferating number of subcommittees."

A non-leadership organization, the Democratic Study Group, is by far the most useful to investigators. The DSG churns out numerous publications for its 200 House members and makes them easily available. One congressional committee aide called DSG materials "the primary source of current legislative research for members of Congress and their staffs." DSG's twenty staffers are based in one of the House office buildings. Their salaries are paid with money from subscriptions to DSG publications, plus office funds contributed by congressmen who belong to DSG. Most of the time, investigators use DSG material as background. But occasionally a DSG publication will be quoted directly, as when Dick Kirschten of the *National Journal* reported the Democratic group was complaining about a "gag rule" imposed by the Reagan administration on agency experts concerning budget cuts.

The main DSG publications are the "Legislative Report," a detailed look at bills scheduled for House consideration during the following week; the "Staff Bulletin," a weekly divided into eight sections (upcoming legislation, important bills reported by committees, selected hearings and markups, legislative proposals being circulated by individual members, references to useful articles from the *Congressional Record* and elsewhere, references to important *Federal Register* items, examples of members' responses to mail on controversial issues and job openings in congressional offices); the "Daily Report," which lists anticipated amendments to bills scheduled for floor debate; and the "Fact Sheet," a twice monthly detailed look at one bill.

The Congressional Campaign Committees

Democrats and Republicans in the House and in the Senate all have organizations to work for their members' re-election and help candidates of their party beat opposing incumbents. Most Washington correspondents are only vaguely aware of the four campaign committees, all located in offices near the Capitol, despite the useful sources there. David Broder, *Washington Post* political reporter-columnist, is one of the exceptions.

"The Senate and House campaign committees provide good information, especially in the even-numbered years," Broder said. "Polling from the states is available, and the field staff can tell you how a race is shaping up."

Art Wiese, Washington Bureau chief of the *Houston Post*, interviewed staffers at the Democratic Congressional Campaign Committee and the National Republican Congressional Committee for a 1980 story on the re-election prospects for House incumbents. A staffer at the Republican organization told Wiese that powerful veteran Democrats had been targeted for defeat "simply because they're the ones who are vulnerable. They're the ones who go home to their districts the least frequently and who get caught up in being powerful here in Washington and ignore their constituents."

As of 1981, the National Republican Congressional Committee was by far the most sophisticated of the four campaign organizations. Its publications included *Congress Today*, a slick magazine; *Eighty Two*, a periodic primer telling Republican candidates how to run successfully for Congress; and *House Counsel*, sent to anyone who contributed more than $2500. The publications are sometimes shrilly partisan, but are worth reading. An investigator browsing the April 1980 issue of *Congress Today* could have learned about the committee's Advertising School, which trains producers who are later assigned "to Republican House races across the country, (where they are) responsible for producing the media campaigns of dozens of GOP congressional candidates."

The article would have been a tip-off to the extensive campaign services provided to Republican congressional candidates. An investigator would be doing a shoddy job of covering a congressional race without examining the committee's role. As Broder noted in the *Washington Post* while profiling Executive Director Nancy Sinnott, "she will be running a staff of forty people and managing a budget of more than $35 million in the two-year effort Republicans will make to end the Democratic majority in the House in 1982."

From the committee, an investigator can perhaps learn which Democrats have been targeted for defeat in the next election, how much money and what sorts of media services the committee plans to give to its Republican candidates, district by district polling data and much more.

The National Republican Senatorial Committee is not quite so active, but investigators, when they have looked, have found much of interest there, too. Jerry Landauer of the *Wall Street Journal* reported in 1980 that the committee was offering "personal relationships" with senators to those who contributed $1000 or more. Landauer said the donors were promised "give-and-take meetings at private buffets. . .a confidential telephone number providing a clear channel of communication to every

GOP senator and substantive information about what is going on in Congress."

The campaign committees file reports at the Federal Election Commission which disclose what they have raised and spent for candidates. Bill Peterson of the *Washington Post* reported that during 1979-80 the House Republican campaign committee raised $27 million and the Senate GOP committee $20.5 million. In contrast, their Democratic counterparts raised just $1.7 million and $2 million.

Despite those relatively paltry sums, the Democratic Congressional Campaign Committee and the Democratic Senatorial Campaign Committee should not be ignored by investigators. During 1980, the House committee published monthly reports on New Right organizations such as the National Conservative Political Action Committee and the Moral Majority. Those reports pulled together information that would have taken an investigator days or weeks to find. The Democratic House & Senate Council, which raises funds for the campaign committees, publishes a sometimes useful monthly newsletter, *Council Cloakroom*. In addition, an investigator interested in information about Republicans can ask to see the Democratic campaign committees' opposition research.

The National Party Committees

The Republican National Committee and Democratic National Committee have vast resources for investigators who know what to ask for. In a congressional race, the involvement of the national committee and its respective congressional campaign committees sometimes overlap. But the national committees have a much broader scope than the congressional entities—they help candidates for president, vice president and state legislatures as well as for Congress. Furthermore, the national committees set party policy on issues; the House and Senate committees concern themselves very little with policy.

A national committee tends to be handmaiden to the president when its party occupies the White House. After Democratic losses in 1980, insiders criticized the national committee for doing little more than President Carter's bidding. Jules Witcover of the *Washington Star* reported that after the disastrous election the committee "received a bill for $400,000 for late polling by Patrick Caddell, the Carter campaign's pollster, as part of an overall bill from Caddell of more than $3 million." Despite having an incumbent in the White House, the Democratic National Committee raised just $15 million from individual donors during 1979-80, compared to the Republican National Committee's $61 million—so arguments about how the money was spent appeared justified.

Partly as a result of the bickering, the election of a new chairman for the Democratic National Committee was an especially big story in early 1981. Broder, Witcover and Germond wrote repeatedly about Charles Manatt's victory and his plans for revitalizing the committee. An alert investigator would have noted, though, that others were elected to lower Democratic National Committee posts—persons who could be sources in the future. For example, Lynn Cutler, a county supervisor from Iowa, was elected as one of three vice chairpersons. Washington correspondents for Iowa's newspapers passed up a good opportunity for inside information if they failed to cultivate Cutler.

In fact, there are sources galore at the Democratic National Committee. Its 367 members meet at least twice a year and its thirty-three member executive committee meets at least four times annually. In addition, there are dozens of full-time professional staffers. The publications those staffers prepare include the *Democrats' Report,* a monthly newsletter; periodic newsletters aimed at specific Democrats who are black, Hispanic, Asian-American or otherwise ethnic; and profiles of opposition Republican politicians, including a cataloguing of their public statements. Every investigator should have the party's platform, which can be obtained from the national committee, to compare the party's promises to its actual performance.

The Republican National Committee is a similar resource for investigators. At the beginning of 1981, the consensus among political reporters was that the Republican committee was more useful than the Democratic committee. Its monthly magazine *First Monday* contained occasionally interesting articles. The quarterly journal *Common Sense* carried thought-provoking pieces on issues from a Republican perspective. *Public Opinion Report* summarized polling data from across the country, whether it reflected well on Republicans or not. *Talking Points* provided party-line responses to Republican opponents on a variety of issues.

Under its new chairman Richard Richards, elected in 1981, the Republican National Committee became involved in the redistricting of House seats undertaken every ten years by the state legislatures. Adam Clymer of the *New York Times* reported that the committee would spend $1 million on the effort, which the *Washington Post's* Broder said would mean "control of a decade's worth of legislation."

Broder said he stays in touch with field operatives of the national committees because he is unable to travel outside of Washington as much as he would like. "The field people move across the country and come back to Washington," he said. "They're basically reporters. If you're working in Washington for an Oregon newspaper and you want to know if Al Ullman [a powerful Oregon congressman who was upset in 1980] is really in trouble, talk to the field person from that area. You won't get just upbeat talk; these people have their credibility to consider." Broder also gleans information about local races by talking to journalists from that area, by questioning members of Congress and their staffs about what is happening back home and by reading local newspapers. He tries to maintain a broad perspective by cultivating political scientists at think tanks such as the Brookings Institution and the American Enterprise Institute for Public Policy Research as well as lawyers and other sources from the party out of power.

(An investigator will find additional sources at party groups loosely affiliated with the national committees, such as the National Federation of Republican Women, the Republican Governors' Association, the Woman's National Democratic

Club and the Democratic State Chairmen's Association, to name a few.)

Every four years, an investigator needs to be in touch with sources at the national committees because of the presidential nominating conventions, for which the parties receive public funds—$4.4 million each in 1980.

If an investigator needs historical election data, the national committees may be the best bet. The Republican National Committee, for instance, publishes a book every two years with such data. The *1979 Republican Almanac,* a bulky 675 pages, contains a county-by-county breakdown for every state on races for governor and lower statewide offices, as well as for U.S. senator. House races are broken out by congressional district.

The Campaign Consultants

An investigator covering the campaign of an individual candidate is more likely to get inside information from a political consultant than from the Democratic or Republican party organizations—there is a new style of campaigning characterized by the decline of the party and the rise of candidate-centered technology.

The new way is not really brand new. President Dwight Eisenhower hired a television advisor in the early 1950s and used direct mail experts to help him raise money. John Kennedy hired Louis Harris as his pollster in the 1960 presidential race. A *National Journal* survey in 1970 of candidates for the Senate showed that of the sixty-seven who had opposition, all but five used advertising firms, nearly half employed media consultants, more than one-third had pollsters and many hired public relations firms. One political scientist has listed twenty-eight kinds of specialists employed by campaigns.

Writing in a 1980 issue of the magazine *Campaigns & Elections,* Robert Agranoff quotes an expert about 1978 House and Senate races: "The single most clear-cut difference between winners and losers lay in what they did during the early months to plan strategies and ways to carry them out. . .On the whole, those campaigns in which the candidate did not become involved in day-to-day operations tended to succeed. Those in which he did act in a managerial capacity suffered from internal conflicts and tended not to succeed," the expert said.

Nicholas Lemann of the *Washington Post* said "the political industry in 1980 was essential to the fortunes of every major candidate." In the *Washington Post* book titled *The Pursuit of the Presidency 1980,* Lemann noted that top races "pitted consultant versus consultant. . .A consultant who was hot could lend instant legitimacy to a campaign, bringing the candidate who had hired him the serious attention of the press and the political action committees."

The consultants do not fold up their tents three years out of four. Several hundred people are involved in the business all year, every year. In 1981, *Washington Post* reporters Glenn Frankel and Donald Baker profiled an upcoming battle for governor of Virginia. Democrat Charles Robb had hired media consultant Bob Squier, pollster Peter Hart and campaign manager David Doak, all big names in the industry. Republican Marshall Coleman, according to Frankel and Baker, had hired "pollster Richard Wirthlin, who worked for the Reagan-Bush ticket, and Bailey Deardourff & Associates, a political consulting firm whose Republican clients won eleven of twelve races last year, including governorships in Missouri, Indiana and Delaware" and a hotly contested House race in Northern Virginia.

An investigator interested in the 1982 Ohio Senate race need not have waited until that year to start reporting on the reelection chances of liberal Democrat Howard Metzenbaum. By talking to political consultants in early 1981, an investigator could get inside dope—exactly what Jack Germond and Jules Witcover of the *Washington Star* did. They reported that a poll by Robert Teeter showed conservative Governor James Rhodes trailing Metzenbaum by "a substantial margin."

To learn which consultants are working in a campaign, an investigator usually can ask the candidate. If that fails, sources at the congressional campaign committees or national party committees will probably know. Lists exist, too; during the 1980 races, *Campaigns & Elections* published a state-by-state directory of U.S. Senate candidates and their consultants. The Campaign Works—a firm based in Kansas City—publishes *Profile,* "the first national directory of political consultants." Each loose-leaf page shows whether the consultant serves only Democrats, only Republicans, or both; his specialties (for example, direct mail, opposition research or media); and his major clients.

Like most sources, consultants generally can be persuaded to discuss what they do and how they do it. As the *Post's* Lemann said, "People in the political industry like to talk about campaigns as if they were works of art, and to argue about which one was the most perfect."

'PRETTY SOON WE'LL HAVE THE PRESS TOO SCARED TO CRITICIZE ANYONE--INCLUDING US!'

Appendices

Appendix 1

The Washington Correspondents: Whom They Work For

ewspapers headquartered outside Washington, D.C. Most of the nation's 1700 or so dailies have no Washington coverage of their own, especially the smaller papers—and about 70 percent of all American dailies have circulations under 25,000. Only a handful of the under-25,000 group employ a correspondent in Washington to write exclusively for their readership. Smaller dailies that are part of chains may have a Washington correspondent, but rarely is he able to devote full-time coverage to stories of special interest to any one paper. For example, the *Iowa City* (Iowa) *Press-Citizen*, part of the Gannett Company chain, had a reporter in the Washington bureau at the end of 1980. That reporter, however, also reported for Gannett dailies in Kansas, Missouri and Nebraska. Still another chain bureau had three reporters trying to serve thirty-two dailies, three weeklies, four radio and two television stations.

A few dailies like the *Anniston* (Alabama) *Star* paid a stringer who spent at least half of his time on stories localized to the readership. At the start of 1981, about 130 newspapers in twenty-two states had signed on with States News Service, which provided them with targeted Washington coverage for a set weekly payment.

Most dailies, though, do nothing except run stories with Washington datelines from the Associated Press, United Press International or a supplemental wire service such as the Los Angeles Times, Washington Post or Knight-Ridder. The vast majority of the 8000 or so weekly newspapers have no Washington coverage, period. At the other extreme are the few dailies, mostly large, whose teams of Washington correspondents serve no one else. The *New York Times*, *Chicago Tribune* and *Los Angeles Times* are obvious examples. Less well-known nationally are papers like the *Des Moines Register*, which at the start of 1981 had four reporters, two editorial writers and a columnist in its Washington bureau.

• Broadcast stations outside Washington, D.C. As with daily newspapers, most broadcast stations have no pinpointed coverage from Washington, D.C. In 1980, researcher Edmund Lambeth of Indiana University discovered that only seventy to eighty Washington correspondents cover the federal government for about 150 television stations of the approximately 1000 stations across the country. Other researchers estimate an even smaller percentage of radio stations have their own Washington correspondents.

Stations that do have correspondents often share them with other stations in the group. For example, in 1981, Cox Broadcasting had two reporters and two camera crews in its Washington bureau to service five television stations. It had one reporter to handle five AM radio stations. The five major market television stations owned by Columbia Broadcasting System shared one reporter. As with daily newspapers, individual broadcast stations have employees reporting just for them. But those stations are rare. Individual stations employing stringers are rare, too.

There are freelance bureaus, akin to States News Service on the print side. Perhaps the largest is Capital Broadcast News. In 1981, its four reporters and two camera crews sent localized stories to about fifty television stations. Another freelance bureau—with three reporters and two cameramen—had about forty clients, but some bought just a couple of pieces each year. Almost all of the clients were TV stations; the bureau did little work for radio.

When the majority of the country's broadcast stations use news from Washington, it comes by way of the wire services or Washington correspondents of the huge national networks. For instance, WKXO-AM in Berea, Kentucky, is part of the Mutual Broadcasting System so the station receives the five-minute newscasts of Mutual and any special programming from Washington. But Mutual's emphasis is decidedly national; there is no intentional localization.

• National wire services and networks. Everybody has heard of Associated Press and United Press International, of the Columbia Broadcasting System, American Broadcasting Co. and National Broadcasting Co. There are networks and wire services with large Washington operations that are not quite as well-known. It is from these well-known and not so well-known services and networks that most American news media receive their Washington coverage. Some of the operations serve only one medium—just radio, or just television. Others serve print and broadcast outlets. at UPI, for example, there were sixty print professionals in 1981. Of those, forty-four were reporteres and sixteen were editors. Most of the reporters had an institutional beat— the White House, the Senate, Cabinet departments. A few were specialists with beats that cut across institutional lines—science, energy, religion. UPI had no regional reporters serving particular client newspapers, but it occasionally produced localized stories on request.

There were six UPI national audio network reporters covering beats in 1981; once in awhile a print reporter does radio reports. UPI also had three professionals in its Washington Capitol News Service, which supplies a listing of daily events and summaries of national and international news to hundreds of clients in the Washington area. Associated Press had about eighty news professionals in its bureau at the start of 1981, and provided similar services to those of UPI. AP, however, did have eight reporters in the bureau who served specific states.

ABC, CBS and NBC all had Washington bureaus of over 100 persons, but the majority were editors, producers and camera crew members. In 1981, ABC had thirty-one reporters and CBS had twenty-seven. NBC refused to discuss numbers. Each network also had radio reporters. Non-commercial broadcast station groups have Washington bureaus that send mostly national stories to members across the country. Numerous other wire services and networks have Washington operations. For example, Reuters and Agence France-Presse are best-known for international coverage but they staff domestic news beats, too; Cable News Network serves cable television systems with a sizable Washington bureau; the Independent Television News Association sends mostly national stories to stations unaffiliated with ABC, CBS or NBC.

• Periodicals. Most magazines and newsletters have no reason for Washington bureaus because they carry little news about the federal government. But some periodicals have a presence in Washington. *Hudson's Washington News Media Contacts Directory*, a local publication updated quarterly, listed 2773 news outlets here in its 1981 edition—including hundreds of periodicals with headquarters or bureaus in the capital. The directory lists periodicals under eighty-eight subject headings, such as "tires and rubber" and "science." *Time* and *Newsweek* have large bureaus. *U.S. News and World Report*, the third national news weekly, has its headquarters in Washington. The Bureau of National Affairs, also headquartered in Washington, publishes dozens of newsletters covering the legal, economic, labor, tax, financial, environmental, safety and energy realms. *Congressional Quarterly Weekly Report* covers Congress in-depth; the *National Journal* concentrates on the executive branch. Reporters for hundreds of highly specialized newsletters and magazines scour the city for inside information of little general interest but of great import to their own subscribers, be they television station owners, Wall Street brokers or physicians. The specialized publications are read by many investigators for background tips.

• Freelancers. Numbers are impossible to come by. There is an organization of freelancers in Washington, D.C. called Washington Independent Writers; in 1981 it had about 1000 members paying $35 annually. But many freelancers have never joined the group. Some Washington reporters freelance full-time and make a living at it. Their work appears in daily newspapers, magazines, specialized newsletters and publications of government agencies. Many other freelancers have full-time media or non-media jobs and sell articles occasionally to supplement their income or to build their file of clippings.

• Foreign journalists. The Foreign Press Center, run by the U.S. International Communication Agency, listed about 450 resident foreign correspondents from fifty-four nations working in Washington in 1981. Japanese media had at least ninety journalists here according to a recent count. The presence of foreign journalists is expecially noticeable at the State Department, where, at the end of 1980, about 55 percent of the accredtied correspondents were from countries other than America.

• Others. There are other categories of reporters who are very much a part of the Washington scene. The *Washington Post, Washington Star* and suburban dailies and weeklies cover the federal government and also the special interests surrounding the government. Local radio and television stations reporters can often be found on Capitol Hill, at the White House or at the Supreme Court. When photographs are needed, there are photographers ready at the wire services, in individual newspaper and magazine bureaus, at local publications and at freelance services.

Appendix 2

Government in the Sunshine Act (90 Stat. 1241; 5 U.S.C. 552b)

§ 552b. Open meetings.

(a) For purposes of this section—

(1) the term "agency" means any agency, as defined in section 552(e) of this title, headed by a collegial body composed of two or more individual members, a majority of whom are appointed to such position by the President with the advice and consent of the Senate, and any subdivision thereof authorized to act on behalf of the agency;

(2) the term "meeting" means the deliberations of at least the number of individual agency members required to take action on behalf of the agency where such deliberations determine or result in the joint conduct or disposition of official agency business, but does not include deliberations required or permitted by subsection (d) or (e); and

(3) the term "member" means an individual who belongs to a collegial body heading an agency.

(b) Members shall not jointly conduct or dispose of agency business other than in accordance with this section. Except as provided in subsection (c), every portion of every meeting of an agency shall be open to public observation.

(c) Except in a case where the agency finds that the public interest requires otherwise, the second sentence of subsection (b) shall not apply to any portion of an agency meeting, and the requirements of subsections (d) and (e) shall not apply to any information pertaining to such meeting otherwise required by this section to be disclosed to the public, where the agency properly determines that such portion or portions of its meeting or the disclosure of such information is likely to—

(1) disclose matters that are (A) specifically authorized under criteria established by an Executive order to be kept secret in the interests of national defense or foreign policy and (B) in fact properly classified pursuant to such Executive order;

(2) relate solely to the internal personnel rules and practices of an agency;

(3) disclose matters specifically exempted from disclosure statute (other than section 552 of this title), provided that such statute (A) requires that the matters be withheld from the public in such a manner as to leave no discretion on the issue, or (B) establishes particular criteria for withholding or refers to particular types of matters to be withheld;

(4) disclose trade secrets and commercial or financial information obtained from a person and privileged or confidential;

(5) involve accusing any person of a crime, or formally censuring any person;

(6) disclose information of a personal nature where disclosure would constitute a clearly unwarranted invasion of personal privacy;

(7) disclose investigatory records compiled for law enforcement purposes, or information which if written would be contained in such records, but only to the extent that the production of such records or information would (A) interfere with enforcement proceedings, (B) deprive a person of a right to a fair trial or an impartial adjudication, (C) constitute an unwarranted invasion of personal privacy, (D) disclose the identity of a confidential source and, in

the case of a record compiled by a criminal law enforcement authority in the course of a criminal investigation, or by an agency conducting a lawful national security intelligence investigation, confidential information furnished only by the confidential source, (E) disclose investigative techniques and procedures, or (F) endanger the life or physical safety of law enforcement personnel;

(8) disclose information contained in or related to examination, operating, or condition reports prepared by, on behalf of, or for the use of an agency responsible for the regulation or supervision of financial institutions;

(9) disclose information the premature disclosure of which would—

(A) in the case of an agency which regulates currencies, securities, commodities, or financial institutions, be likely to (i) lead to significant financial speculation in currencies, securities, or commodities, or (ii) significantly endanger the stability of any financial institution; or

(B) in the case of any agency, be likely to significantly frustrate implementation of a proposed agency action;

except that subparagraph (B) shall not apply in any instance where the agency has already disclosed to the public the context or nature of its proposed action, or where the agency is required by law to make such disclosure on its own initiative prior to taking final agency action on such proposal; or

(10) specifically concern the agency's issuance of a subpena, or the agency's participation in a civil action or proceeding, an action in a foreign court or international tribunal, or an arbitration, or the initiation, conduct, or disposition by the agency of a particular case of formal agency adjudication pursuant to the procedures in section 554 of this title or otherwise involving a determination on the record after opportunity for a hearing.

(d)(1) Action under subsection (c) shall be taken only when a majority of the entire membership of the agency (as defined in subsection (a)(1)) votes to take such action. A separate vote of the agency members shall be taken with respect to each agency meeting a portion or portions of which are proposed to be closed to the public pursuant to subsection (c), or with respect to any information which is proposed to be withheld under subsection (c). A single vote may be taken with respect to a series of meetings, a portion or portions of which are proposed to be closed to the public, or with respect to any information concerning such series of meetings, so long as each meeting in such series involves the same particular matters and is scheduled to be held no more than thirty days after the initial meeting in such series. The vote of each agency member participating in such vote shall be recorded and no proxies shall be allowed.

(2) Whenever any person whose interests may be directly affected by a portion of a meeting requests that the agency close such portion to the public for any of the reasons referred to in paragraph (5), (6), or (7) of subsection (c), the agency, upon request of any one of its members, shall vote by recorded vote whether to close such meeting.

(3) Within one day of any vote taken pursuant to paragraph (1) or (2), the agency shall make publicly available a written copy of such vote reflecting the vote of each member on the question. If a portion of a meeting is to be closed to the public, the agency shall, within one day of the vote taken pursuant to paragraph (1) or (2) of this subsection, make publicly available a full written explanation of its action closing the portion together with a list of all persons expected to attend the meeting and their affiliation.

(4) Any agency, a majority of whose meetings may properly be closed to the public pursuant to paragraph (4), (8), (9)(A), or (10) of subsection (c), or any combination thereof, may provide by regulation for the closing of such meetings

or portions thereof in the event that a majority of the members of the agency votes recorded vote at the beginning of such meeting, or portion thereof, to close the exempt portion or portions of the meeting, and a copy of such vote, reflecting the vote of each member on the question, is made available to the public. The provisions of paragraphs (1), (2), and (3) of this subsection and subsection (e) shall not apply to any portion of a meeting to which such regulations apply: *Provided,* That the agency shall, except to the extent that such information is exempt from disclosure under the provisions of subsection (c), provide the public with public announcement of the time, place, and subject matter of the meeting and of each portion thereof at the earliest practicable time.

(e) (1) In the case of each meeting, the agency shall make public announcement, at least one week before the meeting, of the time, place, and subject matter of the meeting, whether it is to be open or closed to the public, and the name and phone number of the official designated by the agency to respond to requests for information about the meeting. Such announcement shall be made unless a majority of the members of the agency determines by a recorded vote that agency business requires that such meeting be called at an earlier date, in which case the agency shall make public announcement of the time, place, and subject matter of such meeting, and whether open or closed to the public, at the earliest practicable time.

(2) The time or place of a meeting may be changed following the public announcement required by paragraph (1) only if the agency publicly announces such change at the earliest practicable time. The subject matter of a meeting, or the determination of the agency to open or close a meeting, or portion of a meeting, to the public, may be changed following the public announcement required by this subsection only if (A) a majority of the entire membership of the agency determines by a recorded vote that agency business so requires and that no earlier announcement of the change was possible, and (B) the agency publicly announces such change and the vote of each member upon such change at the earliest practicable time.

(3) Immediately following each public announcement required by this subsection, notice of the time, place, and subject matter of a meeting, whether the meeting is open or closed, any change in one of the preceding, and the name and phone number of the official designated by the agency to respond to requests for information about the meeting, shall also be submitted for publication in the Federal Register.

(f) (1) For every meeting closed pursuant to paragraphs (1) through (10) of subsection (c), the General Counsel or chief legal officer of the agency shall publicly certify that, in his or her opinion, the meeting may be closed to the public and shall state each relevant exemptive provision. A copy of such certification, together with a statement from the presiding officer of the meeting setting forth the time and place of the meeting, and the persons present, shall be retained by the agency. The agency shall maintain a complete transcript or electronic recording adequate to record fully the proceedings of each meeting, or portion of a meeting, closed to the public, except that in the case of a meeting, or portion of a meeting, closed to the public pursuant to paragraph (8), (9) (A), or (10) of subsection (c), the agency shall maintain either such a transcript or recording, or a set of minutes. Such minutes shall fully and clearly describe all matters discussed and shall provide a full and accurate summary of any actions taken, and the reasons therefor, including a description of each of the views expressed on any item and the record of any rollcall vote (reflecting the vote of each member on the question). All documents considered in connection with any action shall be identified in such minutes.

(2) The agency shall make promptly available to the public, in a place easily accessible to the public, the transcript, electronic recording, or minutes (as required by paragraph (1)) of the discussion of any item on the agenda, or of any item of the testimony of any witness received at the meeting, except for such item or items of such discussion or testimony as the agency determines to contain information which may be withheld under subsection (c). Copies of such transcript, or minutes, or a transcription of such recording disclosing the identity of each speaker, shall be furnished to any person at the actual cost of duplication or transcription. The agency shall maintain a complete verbatim copy of the transcript, a complete copy of the minutes, or a complete electronic recording of each meeting, or portion of a meeting, closed to the public, for a period of at least two years after such meeting, or until one year after the conclusion of any agency proceeding with respect to which the meeting or portion was held, whichever occurs later.

(g) Each agency subject to the requirements of this section shall, within 180 days after the date of enactment of this section, following consultation with the Office of the Chairman of the Administrative Conference of the United States and published notice in the Federal Register of at least thirty days and opportunity for written comment by any person, promulgate regulations to implement the requirements of subsections (b) through (f) of this section. Any person may bring a proceeding in the United States District Court for the District of Columbia to require an agency to promulgate such regulations if such agency has not promulgated such regulations within the time period specified herein. Subject to any limitations of time provided by law, any person may bring a proceeding in the United States Court of Appeals for the District of Columbia to set aside agency regulations issued pursuant to this subsection that are not in accord with the requirements of subsections (b) through (f) of this section and to require the promulgation of regulations that are in accord with such subsections.

(h)(1) The district courts of the United States shall have jurisdiction to enforce the requirements of subsections (b) through (f) of this section by declaratory judgment, injunctive relief, or other relief as may be appropriate. Such actions may be brought by any person against an agency prior to, or within sixty days after, the meeting out of which the violation of this section arises, except that if public announcement of such meeting is not initially provided by the agency in accordance with the requirements of this section, such action may be instituted pursuant to this section at any time prior to sixty days after any public announcement of such meeting. Such actions may be brought in the district court of the United States for the district in which the agency meeting is held or in which the agency in question has its headquarters, or in the District Court for the District of Columbia. In such actions a defendant shall serve his answer within thirty days after the service of the complaint. The burden is on the defendant to sustain his action. In deciding such cases the court may examine in camera any portion of the transcript, electronic recording, or minutes of a meeting closed to the public, and may take such additional evidence as it deems necessary. The court, having due regard for orderly administration and the public interest, as well as the interests of the parties, may grant such equitable relief as it deems appropriate, including granting an injunction against future violations of this section or ordering the agency to make available to the public such portion of the transcript, recording, or minutes of a meeting as is not authorized to be withheld under subsection (c) of this section.

(2) Any Federal court otherwise authorized by law to review agency action may, at the application of any person properly participating in the proceeding pursuant to other applicable law, inquire into violations by the agency of the

requirements of this section and afford such relief as it deems appropriate. Nothing in this section authorizes any Federal court having jurisdiction solely on the basis of paragraph (1) to set aside, enjoin, or invalidate any agency action (other than an action to close a meeting or to withhold information under this section) taken or discussed at any agency meeting out of which the violation of this section arose.

(i) The court may assess against any party reasonable attorney fees and other litigation costs reasonably incurred by any other party who substantially prevails in any action brought in accordance with the provisions of subsection (g) or (h) of this section, except that costs may be assessed against the plaintiff only where the court finds that the suit was initiated by the plaintiff primarily for frivolous or dilatory purposes. In the case of assessment of costs against an agency, the costs may be assessed by the court against the United States.

(j) Each agency subject to the requirements of this section shall annually report to Congress regarding its compliance with such requirements, including a tabulation of the total number of agency meetings open to the public, the total number of meetings closed to the public, the reasons for closing such meetings, and a description of any litigation brought against the agency under this section, including any costs assessed against the agency in such litigation (whether or not paid by the agency).

(k) Nothing herein expands or limits the present rights of any person under section 552 of this title, except that the exemptions set forth in subsection (c) of this section shall govern in the case of any request made pursuant to section 552 to copy or inspect the transcripts, recordings, or minutes described in subsection (f) of this section. The requirements of chapter 33 of title 44, United States Code, shall not apply to the transcripts, recordings, and minutes described in subsection (f) of this section.

(l) This section does not constitute authority to withhold any information from Congress, and does not authorize the closing of any agency meeting or portion thereof required by any other provision of law to be open.

(m) Nothing in this section authorizes any agency to withhold from any individual any record, including transcripts, recordings, or minutes required by this section, which is otherwise accessible to such individual under section 552a of this title.

(Pub. L. 94–409, § 3(a), Sept. 13, 1976, 90 Stat. 1241.)

Appendix 3

Freedom of Information Act (81 Stat. 54; 5 U.S.C. 552), as amended

§ 552. Public information; agency rules, opinions, orders, records, and proceedings.

(a) Each agency shall make available to the public information as follows:

(1) Each agency shall separately state and currently publish in the Federal Register for the guidance of the public—

(A) descriptions of its central and field organization and the established places at which, the employees (and in the case of a uniformed service, the members) from whom, and the methods whereby, the public may obtain information, make submittals or requests, or obtain decisions;

(B) statements of the general course and method by which its functions are channeled and determined, including the nature and requirements of all formal and informal procedures available;

(C) rules of procedure, descriptions of forms available or the places at which the forms may be obtained, and instructions as to the scope and contents of all papers, reports, or examinations;

(D) substantive rules of general applicability adopted as authorized by law, and statements of general policy or interpretations of general applicability formulated and adopted by the agency; and

(E) each amendment, revision, or repeal of the foregoing.

Except to the extent that a person has actual and timely notice of the terms thereof, a person may not in any manner be required to resort to, or be adversely affected by, a matter required to be published in the Federal Register and not so published. For the purpose of this paragraph, matter reasonably available to the class of persons affected thereby is deemed published in the Federal Register when incorporated by reference therein with the approval of the Director of the Federal Register.

(2) Each agency, in accordance with published rules, shall make available for public inspection and copying—

(A) final opinions, including concurring and dissenting opinions, as well as orders, made in the adjudication of cases;

(B) those statements of policy and interpretations have been adopted by the agency and are not published in the Federal Register; and

(C) administrative staff manuals and instructions to staff that affect a member of the public;

unless the materials are promptly published and copies offered for sale. To the extent required to prevent a clearly unwarranted invasion of personal privacy, an agency may delete identifying details when it makes available or publishes an opinion, statement of policy, interpretation, or staff manual or instruction. However, in each case the justification for the deletion shall be explained fully in writing. Each agency shall also maintain and make available for public inspection and copying current indexes providing identifying information for the public as to any matter issued, adopted, or promulgated after July 4, 1967, and required by this paragraph to be made available or published. Each agency shall promptly publish, quarterly or more frequently, and distribute (by sale or otherwise) copies of each index or supplements thereto unless it determines by order published in the Federal Register that the publication would be unnecessary and impracticable, in which case the agency shall nonetheless provide copies of such index on request at a cost not to exceed the direct cost of duplication. A final order, opinion, statement of policy, interpretation, or staff manual or instruction that affects a member of the public may be relied on, used, or cited as precedent by an agency against a party other than an agency only if—

(i) it has been indexed and either made available or published as provided by this paragraph; or

(ii) the party has actual and timely notice of the terms thereof.

(3) Except with respect to the records made available under paragraphs (1) and (2) of this subsection, each agency, upon any request for records which (A) reasonably describes such records and (B) is made in accordance with published rules stating the time, place, fees (if any), and procedures to be followed, shall make the records promptly available to any person.

(4) (A) In order to carry out the provisions of this section, each agency shall promulgate regulations, pursuant to notice and receipt of public comment, specifying a uniform schedule of fees applicable to all constituent units of such agency. Such fees shall be limited to reasonable standard charges for document search and duplication and provide for recovery of only the direct costs of such search and duplication. Documents shall be furnished without charge or at a reduced charge where the agency determines that waiver or reduction of the fee is in the public interest because furnishing the information can be considered as primarily benefiting the general public.

(B) On complaint, the district court of the United States in the district in which the complainant resides, or has his principal place of business, or in which the agency records are situated, or in the District of Columbia, has jurisdiction to enjoin the agency from withholding agency records and to order the production of any agency records improperly withheld from the complainant. In such a case the court shall determine the matter do novo, and may examine the contents of such agency records in camera to determine whether such records or any part thereof shall be withheld under any of the exemptions set forth in subsection (b) of this section, and the burden is on the agency to sustain its action.

(C) Notwithstanding any other provision of law, the defendant shall serve an answer or otherwise plead to any complaint made under this subsection within thirty days after service upon the defendant of the pleading in which such complaint is made, unless the court otherwise directs for good cause shown.

(D) Except as to cases the court considers of greater importance, proceedings before the district court, as authorized by this subsection, and appeals therefrom, take precedence on the docket over all cases and shall be assigned for hearing and trial or for argument at the earliest practicable date and expedited in every way.

(E) The court may assess against the United States reasonable attorney fees and other litigation costs reasonably incurred in any case under this section in which the complainant has substantially prevailed.

(F) Whenever the court orders the production of any agency records improperly withheld from the complainant and assesses against the United States reasonable attorney fees and other litigation costs, and the court additionally issues a written finding that the circumstances surrounding the withholding raise questions whether agency personnel acted arbitrarily or capriciously with respect to the withholding, the Civil Service Commission shall promptly initiate a proceeding to determine whether disciplinary action is warranted against the officer or employee who was primarily responsible for the withholding. The Commission, after investigation and consideration of the evidence submitted shall submit its findings and recommendations to the administrative authority of the agency concerned and shall send copies of the findings and recommedations to the officer or employee or his representative. The administrative authority shall take the corrective action that the Commission recommends.

(G) In the event of noncompliance with the order of the court, the district court may punish for contempt the responsible employee, and in the case of a uniformed service, the responsible member.

(5) Each agency having more than one member shall maintain and make available for public inspection a record of the final votes of each member in every agency proceeding.

(6) (A) Each agency, upon any request for records made under paragraph (1), (2), or (3) of this subsection, shall—

(i) determine within ten days (excepting Saturdays, Sundays, and legal public holidays) after the receipt of any such request whether to comply with such request and shall immediately notify the person making such request of such determination and the reasons therefor, and of the right of such person to appeal to the head of the agency any adverse determination; and

(ii) make a determination with respect to any appeal within twenty days (excepting Saturdays, Sundays, and legal public holidays) after the receipt of such appeal. If on appeal the denial of the request for records is in whole or in part upheld, the agency shall notify the person making such request of the provisions for judicial review of that determination under paragraph (4) of this subsection.

(B) In unusual circumstances as specified in this subparagraph, the time limits prescribed in either clause (i) or clause (ii) of subparagraph (A) may be extended by written notice to the person making such request setting forth the reasons for such extension and the date on which a determination is expected to be dispatched. No such notice shall specify a date that would result in an extension for more than ten working days. As used in this subparagraph, "unusual circumstances" means, but only to the extent reasonably necessary to the proper processing of the particular request—

(i) the need to search for and collect the requested records from field facilities or other establishments that are separate from the office processing the request;

(ii) the need to search for, collect, and appropriately examine a voluminous amount of separate and distinct records which are demanded in a single request; or

(iii) the need for consultation, which shall be conducted with all practicable speed, with another agency having a substantial interest in the determination of the request or among two or more components of the agency having substantial subject-matter interest therein.

(C) Any person making a request to any agency for records under paragraph (1), (2), or (3) of this subsection shall be deemed to have exhausted his administrative remedies with respect to such request if the agency fails to comply with the applicable time limit provisions of this paragraph. If the Government can show exceptional circumstances exist and that the agency is exercising due diligence in responding to the request, the court may retain jurisdiction and allow the agency additional time to complete its review of the records. Upon any determination by an agency to comply with a request for records, the records shall be made promptly available to such person making such request. Any notification of denial of any request for records under this subsection shall set forth the names and titles or positions of each person responsible for the denial of such request.

(b) This section does not apply to matters that are—

(1) (A) specifically authorized under criteria established by an Executive order to be kept secret in the interest of national defense or foreign policy and (B) are in fact properly classified pursuant to such Executive order;

(2) related solely to the internal personnel rules and practices of an agency;

(3) specifically exempted from disclosure by statute (other than section 552b of this title), provided that such statute (A) requires that the matters be withheld from the public in such a manner as to leave no discretion on the issue, or (B) establishes particular criteria for withholding or refers to particular types of matters to be withheld;

(4) trade secrets and commercial or financial information obtained from a person and privileged or confidential;

(5) inter-agency or intra-agency memorandums or letters which would not be available by law to a party other than an agency in litigation with the agency;

(6) personnel and medical files and similar files the disclosure of which would constitute a clearly unwarranted invasion of personal privacy;

(7) investigatory records compiled for law enforcement purposes, but only to the extent that the production of such records would (A) interfere with enforcement proceedings, (B) deprive a person of a right to a fair trial or an impartial adjudication, (C) constitute an unwarranted invasion of personal privacy, (D) disclose the identity of a confidential source and, in the case of a record compiled by a criminal law enforcement authority in the course of a criminal investigation, or by an agency conducting a lawful national security intelligence investigation, confidential information furnished only by the confidential source, (E) disclose investigative techniques and procedures, or (F) endanger the life or physical safety of law enforcement personnel;

(8) contained in or related to examination, operating, or condition reports prepared by, on behalf of, or for the use of an agency responsible for the regulation or supervision of financial institutions; or

(9) geological and geophysical information and data, including maps, concerning wells.

Any reasonably segregable portion of a record shall be provided to any person requesting such record after deletion of the portions which are exempt under this subsection.

(c) This section does not authorize withholding of information or limit the availability of records to the public, except as specifically stated in this section. This section is not authority to withhold information from Congress.

(d) On or before March 1 of each calendar year, each agency shall submit a report covering the preceding calendar year to the Speaker of the House of Representatives and President of the Senate for referral to the appropriate committees of the Congress. The report shall include—

(1) the number of determinations made by such agency not to comply with requests for records made to such agency under subsection (a) and the reasons for each such determination;

(2) the number of appeals made by persons under subsection (a) (6), the result of such appeals, and the reason for the action upon each appeal that results in a denial of information;

(3) the names and titles or positions of each person responsible for the denial of records requested under this section, and the number of instances of participation for each;

(4) the results of each proceeding conducted pursuant to subsection (a)(4)(F), including a report of the disciplinary action taken against the officer or employee who was primarily responsible for improperly withholding records or an explanation of why disciplinary action was not taken;

(5) a copy of every rule made by such agency regarding this section;

(6) a copy of the fee schedule and the total amount of fees collected by the agency for making records available under this section; and

(7) such other information as indicates efforts to administer fully this section.

The Attorney General shall submit an annual report on or before March 1 of each calendar year which shall include for the prior calendar year a listing of the number of cases arising under this section, the exemption involved in each case, the disposition of such case, and the cost, fees, and penalties assessed under subsections (a)(4)(E), (F), and (G). Such report shall also include a description of the efforts undertaken by the Department of Justice to encourage agency compliance with this section.

(e) For purposes of this section, the term "agency" as defined in section 551(1) of this title includes any executive department, military department, Government corporation, Government controlled corporation, or other establishment in the executive branch of the Government (including the Executive Office of the President), or any independent regulatory agency.

(Pub. L. 89–554, Sept. 6, 1966, 80 Stat. 383; Pub. L. 90–23, § 1, June 5, 1967, 81 Stat. 54; Pub. L. 93–502, §§ 1–3, Nov. 21, 1974, 88 Stat. 1561–1564; Pub. L. 94–409, § 5(b), Sept. 13, 1976, 90 Stat. 1247.)

Appendix 4

Privacy Act of 1974 (88 Stat. 1896; 5 U.S.C. 552a), as amended

§ 552a. Records maintained on individuals

(a) DEFINITIONS.—For purposes of this section—

(1) the term "agency" means agency as defined in section 552(e) of this title;

(2) the term "individual" means a citizen of the United States or an alien lawfully admitted for permanent residence;

(3) the term "maintain" includes maintain, collect, use, or disseminate;

(4) the term "record" means any item, collection, or grouping of information about an individual that is maintained by an agency, including, but not limited to, his education, financial transactions, medical history, and criminal or employment history and that contains his name, or the identifying number, symbol, or other identifying particular assigned to the individual, such as a finger or voice print or a photograph;

(5) the term "system of records" means a group of any records under the control of any agency from which information is retrieved by the name of the individual or by some identifying number, symbol, or other identifying particular assigned to the individual;

(6) the term "statistical record" means a record in a system of records maintained for statistical research or reporting purposes only and not used in whole or in part in making any determination about an identifiable individual, except as provided by section 8 of title 13; and

(7) the term "routine use" means, with respect to the disclosure of a record, the use of such record for a purpose which is compatible with the purpose for which it was collected.

(b) CONDITIONS OF DISCLOSURE.—No agency shall disclose any record which is contained in a system of records by any means of communication to any person, or to another agency, except pursuant to a written request by, or with the prior written consent of, the individual to whom the record pertains, unless disclosure of the record would be—

(1) to those officers and employees of the agency which maintains the record who have a need for the record in the performance of their duties;

(2) required under section 552 of this title;

(3) for a routine use as defined in subsection (a)(7) of this section and described under subsection (e)(4)(D) of this section;

(4) to the Bureau of the Census for purposes of planning or carrying out a census or survey or related activity pursuant to the provisions of title 13;

(5) to a recipient who has provided the agency with advance adequate written assurance that the record will be used solely as a statistical research or reporting record, and the record is to be transferred in a form that is not individually identifiable;

(6) to the National Archives of the United States as a record which has sufficient historical or other value to warrant its continued preservation by the United States Government, or for evaluation by the Administrator of General Services or his designee to determine whether the record has such value;

(7) to another agency or to an instrumentality of any governmental jurisdiction within or under the control of the United States for a civil or criminal law enforcement activity if the activity is authorized by law, and if the head of the agency or instrumentality has made a written request to the agency which maintains the record specifying the particular portion desired and the law enforcement activity for which the record is sought;

(8) to a person pursuant to a showing of compelling circumstances affecting the health or safety of an individual if upon such disclosure notification is transmitted to the last known address of such individual;

(9) to either House of Congress, or, to the extent of matter within its jurisdiction, any committee or subcommittee thereof, any joint committee of Congress or subcommittee of any such joint committee;

(10) to the Comptroller General, or any of his authorized representatives, in the course of the performance of the duties of the General Accounting Office; or

(11) pursuant to the order of a court of competent jurisdiction.

(c) ACCOUNTING OF CERTAIN DISCLOSURES.—Each agency, with respect to each system of records under its control, shall—

(1) except for disclosures made under subsections (b)(1) or (b)(2) of this section, keep an accurate accounting of—

(A) the date, nature, and purpose of each disclosure of a record to any person or to another agency made under subsection (b) of this section; and

(B) the name and address of the person or agency to whom the disclosure is made;

(2) retain the accounting made under paragraph (1) of this subsection for at least five years or the life of the record, whichever is longer, after the disclosure for which the accounting is made;

(3) except for disclosures made under subsection (b)(7) of this section, make the accounting made under paragraph (1) of this subsection available to the individual named in the record at his request; and

(4) inform any person or other agency about any correction or notation of dispute made by the agency in accordance with subsection (d) of this section of any record that has been disclosed to the person or agency if an accounting of the disclosure was made.

(d) ACCESS TO RECORDS.—Each agency that maintains a system or records shall—

(1) upon request by any individual to gain access to his record or to any information pertaining to him which is contained in the system, permit him and upon his request, a person of his own choosing to accompany him, to review the record and have a copy made of all or any portion thereof in a form comprehensible to him, except that the agency may require the individual to furnish a written statement authorizing discussion of that individual's record in the accompanying person's presence;

(2) permit the individual to request amendment of a record pertaining to him and—

(A) not later than 10 days (excluding Saturdays, Sundays, and legal public holidays) after the date of receipt of such request, acknowledge in writing such receipt; and

(B) promptly, either—

(i) make any correction of any portion thereof which the individual believes is not accurate, relevant, timely, or complete; or

(ii) inform the individual of its refusal to amend the record in accordance with his request, the reason for the refusal, the procedures established by the agency for the individual to request a review of that refusal by the head of the agency or an officer designated by the head of the agency, and the name and business address of that official;

(3) permit the individual who disagrees with the refusal of the agency to amend his record to request a review of such refusal, and not later than 30 days (excluding Saturdays, Sundays, and legal public holidays) from the date on which the individual requests such review, complete such review and make a final determination unless, for good cause shown, the head of the agency extends such 30-day period; and if, after his review, the reviewing official also refuses to amend the record in accordance with the request, permit the individual to file with the agency a concise statement setting forth the reasons for his disagreement with the refusal of the agency, and notify the individual of the provisions for judicial review of the reviewing official's determination under subsection (g)(1)(A) of this section;

(4) in any disclosure, containing information about which the individual has filed a statement of disagreement, occurring after the filing of the statement under paragraph (3) of this subsection, clearly note any portion of the record which is disputed and provide copies of the statement and, if the agency deems it appropriate, copies of a concise statement of the reasons of the agency for not making the amendments requested, to persons or other agencies to whom the disputed record has been disclosed; and

(5) nothing in this section shall allow an individual access to any information compiled in reasonable anticipation of a civil action or proceeding.

(e) AGENCY REQUIREMENTS.—Each agency that maintains a system of records shall—

(1) maintain in its records only such information about an individual as is relevant and necessary to accomplish a purpose of the agency required to be accomplished by statute or by executive order of the President;

(2) collect information to the greatest extent practicable directly from the subject individual when the information may result in adverse determinations about an individual's rights, benefits, and privileges under Federal programs;

(3) inform each individual whom it asks to supply information, on the form which it uses to collect the information or on a separate form that can be retained by the individual—

(A) the authority (whether granted by statute, or by executive order of the President) which authorizes the solicitation of the information and whether disclosure of such information is mandatory or voluntary;

(B) the principal purpose or purposes for which the information is intended to be used;

(C) the routine uses which may be made of the information, as published pursuant to paragraph (4)(D) of this subsection; and

(D) the effects on him, if any, of not providing all or any part of the requested information;

(4) subject to the provisions of paragraph (11) of this subsection, publish in the Federal Register at least annually a notice of the existence and character of the system of records, which notice shall include—

(A) the name and location of the system;

(B) the categories of individuals on whom records are maintained in the system;

(C) the categories of records maintained in the system;

(D) each routine use of the records contained in the system, including the categories of users and the purpose of such use;

(E) the policies and practices of the agency regarding storage, retrievability, access controls, retention, and disposal of the records;

(F) the title and business address of the agency official who is responsible for the system of records;

(G) the agency procedures whereby an individual can be notified at his request if the system of records contains a record pertaining to him;

(H) the agency procedures whereby an individual can be notified at his request how he can gain access to any record pertaining to him contained in the system of records, and how he can contest its content; and

(I) the categories of sources of records in the system;

(5) maintain all records which are used by the agency in making any determination about any individual with such accuracy, relevance, timeliness, and completeness as is reasonably necessary to assure fairness to the individual in the determination;

(6) prior to disseminating any record about an individual to any person other than an agency, unless the dissemination is made pursuant to subsection (b)(2) of this section, make reasonable efforts to assure that such records are accurate, complete, timely, and relevant for agency purposes;

(7) maintain no record describing how any individual exercises rights guaranteed by the First Amendment unless expressly authorized by statute or by the individual about whom the record is maintained or unless pertinent to and within the scope of an authorized law enforcement activity;

(8) make reasonable efforts to serve notice on an individual when any record on such individual is made available to any person under compulsory legal process when such process becomes a matter of public record;

(9) establish rules of conduct for persons involved in the design, development, operation, or maintenance of any system of records, or in maintaining any record, and instruct each such person with respect to such rules and the requirements of this section, including any other rules and procedures adopted pursuant to this section and the penalties for noncompliance;

(10) establish appropriate administrative, technical, and physical safeguards to insure the security and confidentiality of records and to protect against any anticipated threats or hazards to their security or integrity which could result in substantial harm, embarrassment, inconvenience, or unfairness to any individual on whom information is maintained; and

(11) at least 30 days prior to publication of information under paragraph (4)(D) of this subsection, publish in the Federal Register notice of any new use or intended use of the information in the system, and provide an opportunity for interested persons to submit written data, views, or arguments to the agency.

(f) AGENCY RULES.—In order to carry out the provisions of this section, each agency that maintains a system of records shall promulgate rules, in accordance with the requirements (including general notice) of section 553 of this title, which shall—

(1) establish procedures whereby an individual can be notified in response to his request if any system of records named by the individual contains a record pertaining to him;

(2) define reasonable times, places, and requirements for identifying an individual who requests his record or information pertaining to him before the agency shall make the record or information available to the individual;

(3) establish procedures for the disclosure to an individual upon his request of his record or information pertaining to him, including special procedure, if deemed necessary, for the disclosure to an individual of medical records, including psychological records, pertaining to him;

(4) establish procedures for reviewing a request from an individual concerning the amendment of any record or information pertaining to the individual, for making a determination on the request, for an appeal within the agency of an initial adverse agency determination, and for whatever additional means may be necessary for each individual to be able to exercise fully his rights under this section; and

(5) establish fees to be charged, if any, to any individual for making copies of his record, excluding the cost of any search for and review of the record.

The Office of the Federal Register shall annually compile and publish the rules promulgated under this subsection and agency notices published under subsection (e) (4) of this section in a form available to the public at low cost.

(g) (1) CIVIL REMEDIES.—Whenever any agency

(A) makes a determination under subsection (d) (3) of this section not to amend an individual's record in accordance with his request, or fails to make such review in conformity with that subsection;

(B) refuses to comply with an individual request under subsection (d) (1) of this section;

(C) fails to maintain any record concerning any individual with such accuracy, relevance, timeliness, and completeness as is necessary to assure fairness in any determination relating to the qualifications, character, rights, or opportunities of, or benefits to the individual that may be made on the basis of such record, and consequently a determination is made which is adverse to the individual; or

(D) fails to comply with any other provision of this section, or any rule promulgated thereunder, in such a way as to have an adverse effect on an individual,

the individual may bring a civil action against the agency, and the district courts of the United States shall have jurisdiction in the matters under the provisions of this subsection.

(2) (A) In any suit brought under the provisions of subsection (g) (1) (A) of this section, the court may order the agency to amend the individual's record in accordance with his request or in such other way as the court may direct. In such a case the court shall determine the matter de novo.

(B) The court may assess against the United States reasonable attorney fees and other litigation costs reasonably incurred in any case under this paragraph in which the complainant has substantially prevailed.

(3) (A) In any suit brought under the provisions of subsection (g) (1) (B) of this section, the court may enjoin the agency from withholding the records and order the production to the complainant of any agency records improperly withheld from him. In such a case the court shall determine the matter de novo, and may examine the contents of any agency records in camera to determine whether the records or any portion thereof may be withheld under any of the exemptions set forth in subsection (k) of this section, and the burden is on the agency to sustain its action.

(B) The court may assess against the United States reasonable attorney fees and other litigation costs reasonably incurred in any case under this paragraph in which the complainant has substantially prevailed.

(4) In any suit brought under the provisions of subsection (g) (1) (C) or (D) of this section in which the court determines that the agency acted in a manner which was intentional or willful, the United States shall be liable to the individual in an amount equal to the sum of—

 (A) actual damages sustained by the individual as a result of the refusal or failure, but in no case shall a person entitled to recovery receive less than the sum of $1,000; and

 (B) the costs of the action together with reasonable attorney fees as determined by the court.

(5) An action to enforce any liability created under this section may be brought in the district court of the United States in the district in which the complainant resides, or has his principal place of business, or in which the agency records are situated, or in the District of Columbia, without regard to the amount in controversy, within two years from the date on which the cause of action arises, except that where an agency has materially and willfully misrepresented any information required under this section to be disclosed to an individual and the information so misrepresented is material to establishment of the liability of the agency to the individual under this section, the action may be brought at any time within two years after discovery by the individual of the misrepresentation. Nothing in this section shall be construed to authorize any civil action by reason of any injury sustained as the result of a disclosure of a record prior to September 27, 1975.

(h) RIGHTS OF LEGAL GUARDIANS.—For the purposes of this section, the parent of any minor, or the legal guardian of any individual who has been declared to be incompetent due to physical or mental incapacity or age by a court of competent jurisdiction, may act on behalf of the individual.

(i) (1) CRIMINAL PENALTIES.—Any officer or employee of an agency, who by virtue of his employment or official position, has possession of, or access to, agency records which contain individually identifiable information the disclosure of which is prohibited by this section or by rules or regulations established thereunder, and who knowing that disclosure of the specific material is so prohibited, willfully discloses the material in any manner to any person or agency not entitled to receive it, shall be guilty of a misdemeanor and fined not more than $5,000.

(2) Any officer or employee of any agency who willfully maintains a system of records without meeting the notice requirements of subsection (e) (4) of this section shall be guilty of a misdemeanor and fined not more than $5,000.

(3) Any person who knowingly and willfully requests or obtains any record concerning an individual from an agency under false pretenses shall be guilty of a misdemeanor and fined not more than $5,000.

(j) GENERAL EXEMPTIONS.—The head of any agency may promulgate rules, in accordance with the requirements (including general notice) of sections 553 (b) (1), (2), and (3), (c), and (e) of this title, to exempt any system of records within the agency from any part of this section except subsections (b), (c) (1) and (2), (e) (4) (A) through (F), (e) (6), (7), (9), (10), and (11), and (i) if the system of records is—

 (1) maintained by the Central Intelligence Agency; or

 (2) maintained by an agency or component thereof which performs as its principal function any activity pertaining to the enforcement of criminal laws, including police efforts to prevent, control, or reduce crime or to

apprehend criminals, and the activities of prosecutors, courts, correctional, probation, pardon, or parole authorities, and which consists of '(A) information compiled for the purpose of identifying individual criminal offenders and alleged offenders and consisting only of identifying data and notations of arrests, the nature and disposition of criminal charges, sentencing, confinement, release, and parole and probation status; (B) information compiled for the purpose of a criminal investigation, including reports of informants and investigators, and associated with an identifiable individual; or (C) reports identifiable to an individual compiled at any stage of the process of enforcement of the criminal laws from arrest or indictment through release from supervision.

At the time rules are adopted under this subsection, the agency shall include in the statement required under section 553(c) of this title, the reasons why the system of records is to be exempted from a provision of this section.

(k) SPECIFIC EXEMPTIONS.—The head of any agency may promulgate rules, in accordance with the requirements (including general notice) of sections 553 (b) (1), (2), and (3), (c), and (e) of this title, to exempt any system of records within the agency from subsections (c) (3), (d), (e) (1), (e) (4) (G), (H), and (I) and (f) of this section if the system of records is—

(1) subject to the provisions of section 552(b) (1) of this title;

(2) investigatory material compiled for law enforcement purposes, other than material within the scope of subsection (j) (2) of this section: *Provided however,* That if any individual is denied any right, privilege, or benefit that he would otherwise be entitled by Federal law, or for which he would otherwise be eligible, as a result of the maintenance of such material, such material shall be provided to such individual, except to the extent that the disclosure of such material would reveal the identity of a source who furnished information to the Government under an express promise that the identity of the source would be held in confidence, or, prior to the effective date of this section, under an implied promise that the identity of the source would be held in confidence;

(3) maintained in connection with providing protective services to the President of the United States or other individuals pursuant to section 3056 of title 18;

(4) required by statute to be maintained and used solely as statistical records;

(5) investigatory material compiled solely for the purpose of determining suitability, eligibility, or qualifications for Federal civilian employment, military service, Federal contracts, or access to classified information, but only to the extent that the disclosure of such material would reveal the identity of a source who furnished information to the Government under an express promise that the identity of the source would be held in confidence, or, prior to the effective date of this section, under an implied promise that the identity of the source would be held in confidence;

(6) testing or examination material used solely to determine individual qualifications for appointment or promotion in the Federal service the disclosure of which would compromise the objectivity or fairness of the testing or examination process; or

(7) evaluation material used to determine potential for promotion in the armed services, but only to the extent that the disclosure of such material would reveal the identity of a source who furnished information to the Government under an express promise that the identity of the source would be held in confidence, or, prior to the effective date of this section, under an

implied promise that the identity of the source would be held in confidence. At the time rules are adopted under this subsection, the agency shall include in the statement required under section 553(c) of this title, the reasons why the system of records is to be exempted from a provision of this section.

(l)(1) ARCHIVAL RECORDS.—Each agency record which is accepted by the Administrator of General Services for storage, processing, and servicing in accordance with section 3103 of title 44 shall, for the purposes of this section, be considered to be maintained by the agency which deposited the record and shall be subject to the provisions of this section. The Administrator of General Services shall not disclose the record except to the agency which maintains the record, or under rules established by that agency which are not inconsistent with the provisions of this section.

(2) Each agency record pertaining to an identifiable individual which was transferred to the National Archives of the United States as a record which has sufficient historical or other value to warrant its continued preservation by the United States Government, prior to the effective date of this section, shall, for the purposes of this section, be considered to be maintained by the National Archives and shall not be subject to the provisions of this section, except that a statement generally describing such records (modeled after the requirements relating to records subject to subsections (e)(4)(A) through (G) of this section) shall be published in the Federal Register.

(3) Each agency record pertaining to an identifiable individual which is transferred to the National Archives of the United States as a record which has sufficient historical or other value to warrant its continued preservation by the United States Government, on or after the effective date of this section, shall, for the purposes of this section, be considered to be maintained by the National Archives and shall be exempt from the requirements of this section except subsections (e)(4)(A) through (G) and (e)(9) of this section.

(m) GOVERNMENT CONTRACTORS.—When an agency provides by a contract for the operation by or on behalf of the agency of a system of records to accomplish an agency function, the agency shall, consistent with its authority, cause the requirements of this section to be applied to such system. For purposes of subsection (i) of this section any such contractor and any employee of such contractor, if such contract is agreed to on or after the effective date of this section, shall be considered to be an employee of an agency.

(n) MAILING LISTS.—An individual's name and address may not be sold or rented by an agency unless such action is specifically authorized by law. This provision shall not be construed to require the withholding of names and addresses otherwise permitted to be made public.

(o) REPORT ON NEW SYSTEMS.—Each agency shall provide adequate advance notice to Congress and the Office of Management and Budget of any proposal to establish or alter any system of records in order to permit an evaluation of the probable or potential effect of such proposal on the privacy and other personal or property rights of individuals or the disclosure of information relating to such individuals, and its effect on the preservation of the constitutional principles of federalism and separation of powers.

(p) ANNUAL REPORT.—The President shall submit to the Speaker of the House and the President of the Senate, by June 30 of each calendar year, a consolidated report, separately listing for each Federal agency the number of records contained in any system of records which were exempted from the application of this section under the provisions of subsections (j) and (k) of this section during the preceding calendar year, and the reasons for the exemptions, and such other information as indicates efforts to administer fully this section.

(q) EFFECT OF OTHER LAWS.—No agency shall rely on any exemption contained in section 552 of this title to withhold from an individual any record which is otherwise accessible to such individual under the provisions of this section.

(Pub. L. 93–579, § 3, Dec. 31, 1974, 88 Stat. 1897; Pub. L. 94–183, § 2(2), Dec. 31, 1975, 89 Stat. 1057.)

Bibliography

The books and articles mentioned are quoted or paraphrased in the Introduction and Chapters One through Seven, or were otherwise relied on. Many books and articles have been omitted for reasons of space.

Introduction and Chapter I.

Books

Anderson, David, and Benjaminson, Peter. *Investigative Reporting.* Indiana University Press, 1976.

Anderson, Jack, with Boyd, James. *Confessions of a Muckraker.* Random House, 1979.

Babb, Laura Longley, ed. *Of the Press, by the Press, for the Press (and Others, Too).* Washington Post, 1974.

Bagdikian, Ben. *The Effete Conspiracy.* Harper & Row, 1972.

Blanchard, Robert, ed. *Congress and the News Media.* Hastings House, 1974.

Brady, John. *The Craft of Interviewing.* Vintage Books, 1976.

Bray, Howard. *The Pillars of the Post: The Making of a News Empire in Washington.* Norton, 1980.

Cannon, Lou. *Reporting: An Inside View*. California Journal Press, 1977.

Cater, Douglass. *The Fourth Branch of Government*. Houghton Mifflin, 1959.

Cheshire, Maxine, with Greenya, John. *Maxine Cheshire: Reporter*. Houghton Mifflin, 1978.

Cohen, Bernard. *The Press and Foreign Policy*. Princeton University Press, 1963.

Collier, Barney. *Hope and Fear in Washington (the Early Seventies): The Story of the Washington Press Corps*. Dial Press, 1975.

Crouse, Timothy. *The Boys on the Bus*. Ballantine Books, 1973.

Dickerson, Nancy. *Among Those Present: A Reporter's View of Twenty-Five Years in Washington*. Random House, 1977.

Downie, Leonard Jr. *The New Muckrakers*. New Republic Book Co., 1976.

Dygert, James. *The Investigative Journalist: Folk Heroes of a New Era*. Prentice-Hall, 1976.

Ephron, Nora. *Scribble, Scribble*. Knopf, 1978.

Grossman, Michael, and Kumar, Martha. *Portraying the President: The White House and the News Media*. Johns Hopkins University Press, 1981.

Hess, Stephen. *The Washington Reporters*. Brookings Institution, 1981.

Hiebert, Ray, ed. *The Press in Washington*. Dodd, Mead, 1966.

Krock, Arthur. *Memoirs*. Funk & Wagnalls, 1968.

Lee, Richard, ed. *Politics & the Press*. Acropolis Books, 1970.

Marbut, F.B. *News from the Capital: The Story of Washington Reporting*. Southern Illinois University Press, 1971.

Mollenhoff, Clark. *Investigative Reporting*. Macmillan, 1981.

Nimmo, Dan. *Newsgathering in Washington*. Atherton Press, 1964.

Paletz, David, and Entman, Robert. *Media, Power, Politics*. Free Press, 1981.

Patterson, Thomas. *The Mass Media Election*. Praeger, 1980.

Perry, James. *Us & Them*. Clarkson N. Potter, 1973.

Rather, Dan, with Herskowitz, Mickey. *The Camera Never Blinks*. Ballantine Books, 1977.

Reston, James. *The Artillery of the Press*. Harper & Row, 1966.

Rivers, William. *The Opinionmakers*. Beacon Press, 1965.

Rosten, Leo. *The Washington Correspondents*. Harcourt, Brace, 1937.

Schorr, Daniel. *Clearing the Air*. Houghton Mifflin, 1977.

Sigal, Leon. *Reporters and Officials: The Organization and Politics of Newsmaking*. D.C. Heath, 1973.

Strentz, Herbert. *News Reporters and News Sources*. Iowa State University Press, 1978.

Wicker, Tom. *On Press*. Viking, 1978.

Williams, Paul. *Investigative Reporting and Editing*. Prentice-Hall, 1978.

Articles

Allen, George. "All in the Family: *National Journal* and *Congressional Quarterly*." *Washington Journalism Review*, January-February 1979.

American Enterprise Institute for Public Policy Research. "The Press and Public Policy." AEI Forum, January 1979.

Archibald, S.J. "The Revised FOI Law—and How to Use It." *Columbia Journalism Review*, July-August 1977.

Bagdikian, Ben. "Congress and the Media: Partners in Propaganda." *Columbia Journalism Review*, January-February 1974.

Bryant, Tim. "Freedom of Information Act Useful for Investigative Work." *IRE Journal*, October-November 1978.

Cole, Barry, and Oettinger, Mal. "Covering the Politics of Broadcasting: FCC Commissioners Come and Go, But the Power of the Broadcast Trade Press Endures." *Columbia Journalism Review*, November-December 1977.

Consoli, John. "Reporters Feud Over Issuance of Army Data." *Editors & Publisher*, January 3, 1981.

Dawson, Jim, and Hogan, Bill, with Fletcher, Elizabeth, Klein, Paula and Leavitt, Neal. "The Journalism Establishment." *Washingtonian*, June 1978.

Gup, Ted, and Neumann, Jonathan. "Government Out of Control: Contracts." *Washington Post*, June 22-26, 1980.

Halloran, Richard. "Report on Bomber Disclosure Urges Tight Secrets Law." *New York Times*, February 8, 1981.

Halonen, Doug, Krumm, Jo Ellen, Ludvik, James, Moore, Ann and Seery, Tom. "What Inside Washington Reads." *Washingtonian*, January 1981.

Kiesel, Diane, Nicholson, June, Henkel, John and Fuller-Col, Geri. "Washington Neglected." *The Quill,* May 1978.

Kotz, Nick. "What the *Times* and *Post* Are Missing." *Washington Monthly,* March 1977.

Lambeth, Edmund, and Byrne, John. "Pipelines from Washington." *Columbia Journalism Review,* May-June 1978.

Lambeth, Edmund. "Reporting Washington for Main Street." *Washington Journalism Review,* December 1980.

Lane, Raymond. "The *Wall Street Journal:* Washington's Top Bureau?" *Washington Journalism Review,* January-February 1978.

Lanouette, William. "The Washington Press Corps—Is It All That Powerful?" *National Journal,* June 2, 1979.

McLellan, Joseph. "The Insider's Report—Newsletter Nabobs: An Interest in Special Interests." *Washington Post,* June 24, 1980.

Nessen, Ron. "The Washington You Can't See on Television." *TV Guide,* September 20, 1980.

Obey, David. "Press Fiddles With Perks While Fires Go Unchecked." *Washington Journalism Review,* October, 1977.

O'Reilly, James. "Government in the Sunshine." Freedom of Information Center Report 366, University of Missouri School of Journalism, January 1977.

Randolph, Eleanor. "The Secret Pleasures of the White House Press." *Washington Monthly,* March 1978.

Ranii, David. "The Bureau." *Washington Journalism Review,* April 1981.

Rattner, Steve. "Uncovering Washington." *Brown Alumni Monthly,* December 1980.

Rood, Mick. "Politicking in the Press Corps: Just Like the Real Thing." *Washington Monthly,* April 1979.

Rood, Mick. "Washington's Other Reporters." *Washington Post Magazine,* June 18, 1978.

Rosenberg, John. "Imperiled Experiment: Capitol Hill News Service." *Columbia Journalism Review,* September-October 1977.

Seliger, Susan. "Newsletters: The Fourth and a Half Estate." *Washington Journalism Review,* October 1977.

Shaw, Gaylord. "Reporters Can Save Lives by Investigating Hazards Before They Become Accidents.'" *IRE Journal,* Spring 1980.

Shribman, David. "Sperling's Breakfast Forum." *Washington Star*, February 8, 1981.

Taylor, Jack. "The Freedom of Information Act's Top User Offers Tips on Making This Access Tool Work." *IRE Journal*, Summer 1980.

Weinberg, Steve. "A Gold Mine of Information." *The Bulletin of the American Society of Newspaper Editors*, October 1974.

Weinberg, Steve. "FOI Foiled by a Friend." *Columbia Journalism Review*, November-December 1975.

Weinberg, Steve. "Neal Smith: Small Business Is on His Mind but the Farm Vote Is in His Heart." *Inc.*, September 1980.

Chapter II

Books

Arnold, R. Douglas. *Congress and the Bureaucracy: A Theory of Influence.* Yale University Press, 1979.

Asbell, Bernard. *The Senate Nobody Knows.* Johns Hopkins University Press, 1981.

Baker, Ross. *Friend and Foe in the U.S. Senate.* Free Press, 1980.

Bayh, Marvella, with Kotz, Mary Lynn. *Marvella: A Personal Journey.* Harcourt Brace Jovanovich, 1979.

Bibby, John, Mann, Thomas and Ornstein, Norman. *Vital Statistics on Congress, 1980.* American Enterprise Institute for Public Policy Research, 1980.

Blanchard, Robert, ed. *Congress and the News Media.* Hastings House, 1974.

Clark, Marion, and Maxa, Rudy. *Public Trust, Private Lust: Sex, Power and Corruption on Capitol Hill.* Morrow, 1977.

Congressional Quarterly Inc. *Congressional Ethics.* 1980.

Congressional Quarterly Inc. *Inside Congress,* 1979.

Dodd, Lawrence, and Oppenheimer, Bruce, ed. *Congress Reconsidered.* Congressional Quarterly Press, 1981.

Drew, Elizabeth. *Senator.* Simon and Schuster, 1979.

Fenno, Richard Jr. *Congressmen in Committees.* Little, Brown, 1973.

Fenno, Richard Jr. *Home Style.* Little, Brown, 1978.

Fox, Harrison Jr., and Hammond, Susan. *Congressional Staffs: The Invisible Force in American Lawmaking.* Free Press, 1977.

Groennings, Sven, and Hawley, Jonathan, ed. *To Be a Congressman: The Promise and the Power.* Acropolis Books, 1973.

Hamilton, James. *The Power to Probe.* Vintage Books, 1976.

Havemann, Joel. *Congress and the Budget.* Indiana University Press, 1978.

Jacobson, Gary. *Money in Congressional Elections.* Yale University Press, 1980.

Jones, Rochelle, and Woll, Peter. *The Private World of Congress.* Free Press, 1979.

Malbin, Michael. *Unelected Representatives: A New Role for Congressional Staffs.* Basic, 1980.

Mann, Thomas. *Unsafe at Any Margin: Interpreting Congressional Elections.* American Enterprise Institute for Public Policy Research, 1978.

Mayhew, David. *Congress: The Electoral Connection.* Yale University Press, 1974.

Miller, William, as told to Leighton, Frances. *Fishbait: The Memoirs of the Congressional Doorkeeper.* Prentice-Hall, 1977.

Mollenhoff, Clark. *Investigative Reporting.* Macmillan, 1981.

Oleszek, Walter. *Congressional Procedures and the Policy Process.* Congressional Quarterly Press, 1978.

Ornstein, Norman, ed. *Congress in Change.* Praeger, 1975.

Redman, Eric. *The Dance of Legislation.* Simon and Schuster, 1973.

Reid, T.R. *Congressional Odyssey: The Saga of a Senate Bill.* W.H. Freeman, 1980.

Riegle, Donald, with Armbrister, Trevor. *O Congress.* Popular Library, 1972.

Schick, Allen. *Congress and Money: Budgeting, Spending and Taxing.* Urban Institute, 1980.

Shepsle, Kenneth. *The Giant Jigsaw Puzzle: Democratic Committee Assignments in the Modern House.* University of Chicago Press, 1978.

Tacheron, Donald and Udall, Morris. *The Job of the Congressman.* Bobbs-Merrill, 1966.

Articles

Arieff, Irwin. "More Catholics, Jews, Blacks, Women in Ninety-Seventh Congress." *Congressional Quarterly Weekly Report,* January 24, 1981.

Arieff, Irwin. "State Delegations Strive to Protect Their Interests Through Concerted Effort." *Congressional Quarterly Weekly Report,* August 2, 1980.

Baker, Donald. "Power Broker—Senate Landlord Mathias Exercising His New Clout." *Washington Post,* February 24, 1981.

Bergsten, C. Fred. "Congress' Stalemate System." *New York Times,* January 30, 1981.

Bethell, Thomas. "The Best Job in Washington." *Washington Monthly,* April 1980.

Business Week. "Learning a Fund-Raising Lesson." January 26, 1981.

Dewar, Helen, and Sinclair, Ward. "An Introduction to the Newest Senate Barons." *Washington Post,* January 18, 1981.

Dewar, Helen. "Preserving a Dynasty—Mr. Louisiana Leaves Nothing to Chance." *Washington Post,* September 8, 1980.

Dewar, Helen. "Senate Probe Exposes Fixes in Little Fixup Funds." *Washington Post,* August 30, 1980.

Freedman, Tracy. "Strange Bedfellows: Congressmen Who Own Media." *Washington Journalism Review,* September 1978.

Goodale, John. "Putting Federal Offices Downtown—the Suburbs Are Yelling Foul." *National Journal,* November 15, 1980.

Hall, Carla. "Arts Caucus Formed." *Washington Post,* January 13, 1981.

Halloran, Richard. "Book on Military Finds Avid Readers." *New York Times,* September 28, 1980.

Keller, Bill, and Arieff, Irwin. "As Campaign Costs Skyrocket, Lobbyists Take Growing Role in Washington Fund-Raisers." *Congressional Quarterly Weekly Report,* May 17, 1980.

Landauer, Jerry. "Congressmen Offer Access to Raise Cash." *Wall Street Journal,* August 6, 1980.

Landauer, Jerry. "Shed No Tears for Ex-Lawmakers; They'll Get Some Hefty Pensions." *Wall Street Journal,* November 21, 1980.

Landauer, Jerry. "Travel Caucus Rides in Style on Capitol Hill." *Wall Street Journal,* February 19, 1981.

Lemann, Nicholas. "Fiscal Conservative's District: A Lot of Bucks Stop Here." *Washington Post,* January 29, 1980.

Light, Larry. "Crack Outreach Programs No Longer Ensure Reelection." *Congressional Quarterly Weekly Report,* February 14, 1981.

Malone, Roy, and Rose, Louis. "The Eagletons: Drama of an Embattled Family." *St. Louis Post-Dispatch*, reprinted August 26, 1980 in the *Columbia Missourian*.

Mintz, Morton. "GAO Chief Tells the Pentagon of Fifteen Areas Where It Can Save." *Washington Post*, March 3, 1981.

Nocera, Joseph. "How to Make the Front Page: A Do-It-Yourself Guide for Congressmen." *Washington Monthly*, October 1978.

O'Shea, James, "Obscure Bank Helps Expand Public Debt. *Chicago Tribune*, November 11, 1979.

Pates, James. "Computers Changing Nature of Politics on Capitol Hill."*Fredericksburg (Va.) Free Lance-Star*, December 28, 1978.

Reid, T.R. "Dividing Up the Pie in Fort Wayne, Indiana." *Washington Post*, January 23, 1979.

Rich, Spencer. "Aiding Elderly." *Washington Post*, January 29, 1980.

Rich, Spencer. "Formula Game: Assigning Shares of Federal Funds." *Washington Post*, October 22, 1979.

Riordan, Pat. "Where to Get Started When Investigating Your State's Representative ABSCAM." *IRE Journal*, Spring 1980.

Safire, William. "Madison Group Exerts Political Power Behind the Scene." Syndicated column published in the Columbia Missourian, December 27, 1980.

Samuelson, Robert. "Taking Out a Loan Guarantee." *National Journal*, January 27, 1979.

Schnurer, Eric. "A Slight Oversight: Congress' Space Probe." *Washington Monthly*, November 1979.

Shamer, James. "Changing Congressional Secrecy." Freedom of Information Center Report 330, University of Missouri School of Journalism, November 1974.

Shanahan, Eileen. "Federal Loan Programs Offer Early Test of Reagan Resolve." *Washington Star*, January 14, 1981.

Sinclair, Ward. "Building an Empire—Burton Is Lord of Parks, Territories." *Washington Post*, September 8, 1980.

Sinclair, Ward. "Feeling the Bite in Durham, North Carolina." *Washington Post*, January 23, 1979.

Sinclair, Ward. "NIH Budget Testimony: Reality Lies Between the Lines." *Washington Post*, June 21, 1980.

Sinclair, Ward. "Return of the Free Lunch." *Washington Post*, June 17, 1980.

Sinclair, Ward. "Senator Robert Byrd's History Lessons: Pensive, Extensive and Expensive." *Washington Post,* November 29, 1980.

Stuart, Peter. "Capitol Hill Backs Quietly Away From Reforms of 1970s." *Christian Science Monitor,* February 13, 1981.

Sulzberger, A.O. Jr. "Bumping Heads in the Senate." *New York Times,* June 15, 1980.

Symonds, William. "Environmentalist Culver and the Billboard Industry." *Des Moines Register,* September 21, 1979.

Taylor, Adrian. "The Flacks on the Hill." *Washington Journalism Review,* June-July 1979.

Taylor, Stuart Jr. "Court Bars Curbs on Campaign Work by Congress Aides." *New York Times,* February 4, 1981.

Thornton, Mary, and Hornig, Roberta. "Baker Warns O'Neill on Packing Panels." *Washington Star,* November 14, 1980.

United Press International. "Senate Pays 161 Aides Above $50,000 a Year." *Washington Star,* June 10, 1980.

Weiss, Laura. "Income Grows Despite New House Ceiling." *Congressional Quarterly Weekly Report,* August 23, 1980.

Yank, Andrea. "Congress Sets New Foreign Travel Record." *Congressional Quarterly Weekly Report,* July 26, 1980.

Chapter III

Books

Bernstein, Carl, and Woodward, Bob. *All the President's Men.* Simon and Schuster, 1974.

Bradlee, Benjamin. *Conversations with Kennedy.* Norton, 1975.

Cannon, Lou. *Reporting: An Inside View.* California Journal Press, 1977.

Cohen, Richard, and Witcover, Jules. *A Heartbeat Away.* Bantam, 1974.

Edwards, George III. *Presidential Influence in Congress.* W.H. Freeman, 1980.

Grossman, Michael, and Kumar, Martha. *Portraying the President: The White House and the News Media.* Johns Hopkins University Press, 1981.

Gulley, Bill, with Reese, Mary Ellen. *Breaking Cover.* Simon and Schuster, 1980.

Herbers, John. *No Thank You, Mr. President*. Norton, 1976.

Mollenhoff, Clark. *The President Who Failed*. Macmillan, 1980.

Neustadt, Richard. *Presidential Power: The Politics of Leadership From FDR to Carter*. Wiley, 1980.

Pollard, James. *The Presidents and the Press*. Macmillan, 1974.

Reedy, George. *The Twilight of the Presidency*. Mentor, 1971.

Sussman, Barry. *The Great Cover-up: Nixon and the Scandal of Watergate*. New American Library, 1974.

Talese, Gay. *The Kingdom and the Power*. World Publishing, 1969.

Woodward, Bob and Bernstein, Carl. *The Final Days*. Avon, 1976.

Articles

Associated Press. "Bush, Wife Put Their Assets Into Blind Trust." *Washington Star*, February 14, 1981.

Aug, Stephen. "White House Blocked Conflicting Testimony on Auto Import Issue." *Washington Star*, October 8, 1980.

Billington, Joy. "Projects Emphasize New Role." *Washington Star*, December 21, 1980.

Bonafede, Dom. "The President's Publicity Machine." *Washington Journalism Review*, May 1980.

Broadcasting. "Smooth Sailing So Far for the Brady Bunch." March 16, 1981.

Broder, David. "New Life for an Old Forum." *Washington Post*, February 4, 1981.

Broder, David. "The Way to the Heart of Congress." *Washington Post*, February 1, 1981.

Broder, David. "White House Opens Drive to Sell Governors and Mayors on Fund Cuts." *Washington Post*, February 22, 1981.

Bumiller, Elisabeth. "Brady the Bear Heads for the White House." *Washington Post*, January 12, 1981.

Cannon, Lou. "Nessen's Briefings: Missing Questions (and Answers)." *Columbia Journalism Review*, May-June 1975.

Germond, Jack, and Witcover, Jules. "GOP Still Weak in Many Areas of the South." *Washington Star*, January 8, 1981.

Hirshberg, Jennefer. "Found: An Organized and Unflappable Press Secretary." *Washington Star*, January 12, 1981.

Hyde, John. "Deputy Press Secretary Fights a News Tempest." *Des Moines Register*, February 16, 1981.

Kornheiser, Tony. "Cutting Chaff and Shooting Straight With Jim Baker." *Washington Post,* January 18, 1981.

Lescaze, Lee. "In a Peculiar Twist, Brady Reappears to Brief Press." *Washington Post,* February 15, 1981.

Light, Larry. "White House Domestic Policy Staff Plays An Important Role in Formulating Legislation." *Congressional Quarterly Weekly Report,* October 6, 1979.

Massing, Michael. "Reshuffling the White House Press Pack." *Columbia Journalism Review,* March-April 1981.

Mohr, Charles. "Audit Reports Reagan Committee Exceeded Primary Spending Limits." *New York Times,* February 3, 1981.

O'Leary, Jeremiah. "Elizabeth Dole Gets Post in White House." *Washington Star,* December 21, 1980.

Pound, Edward. "Reagan's Worth Put at $4 Million." *New York Times,* January 23, 1981.

Rogers, Hines III. "Press Secretaries: A Brief Look." Freedom of Information Center Report 386, University of Missouri School of Journalism, March 1978.

Santini, Maureen. "Some Non-political Workers Losing White House Jobs." Associated Press story in the *Washington Post,* January 18, 1981.

Schellhardt, Timothy. "Before Ronald Reagan Chooses, Edwin Meese Sorts Out the Choices." *Wall Street Journal,* February 11, 1981.

Schellhardt, Timothy. "Inflation Complicates Life at 1600 Pennsylvania Avenue." *Wall Street Journal,* July 15, 1980.

Shapiro, Walter. "The Stockman Express," *Washington Post Magazine,* February 8, 1981.

Sidey, Hugh. "Being President Is Not Just Tending the Media." *Washington Star,* February 14, 1981.

Smith, Hedrick. "President Trying to Be Sensitive to Needs of Leaders in Congress." *New York Times,* February 12, 1981.

Smith, Terence. "Kirbo's Home Away From Home Is the Lincoln Bedroom." *New York Times,* June 15, 1980.

Trescott, Jacqueline. "Reagan's Press Team: It's Small's World." *Washington Post,* January 15, 1981.

Weisman, Steven. "Reagan's Role Vital in Personnel Shifts." *New York Times,* February 8, 1981.

Chapter IV.

Books

Downie, Leonard Jr. *The New Muckrakers*. New Republic Book Co., 1976.

Edwards, George III. *Implementing Public Policy*. Congressional Quarterly Press, 1980.

Fritschler, A. Lee. *Smoking and Politics: Policymaking and the Federal Bureaucracy*. Appleton-Century-Crofts, 1969.

Guttman, Daniel, and Willner, Barry. *The Shadow Government*. Pantheon, 1976.

Heclo, Hugh. *A Government of Strangers: Executive Politics in Washington*. Brookings Institution, 1977.

Heise, Juergen. *Minimum Disclosure: Pentagon News Manipulation*. Norton, 1979.

Hess, Stephen. *The Washington Reporters*. Brookings Institution, 1981.

Kalb, Marvin and Bernard. *Kissinger*. Dell, 1974.

Krasnow, Erwin, and Longley, Lawrence. *The Politics of Broadcast Regulation*. St. Martin's, 1978.

Malek, Frederic. *Washington's Hidden Tragedy: The Failure to Make Government Work*. Free Press, 1978.

Ripley, Randall, and Franklin, Grace. *Congress, the Bureaucracy, and Public Policy*. Dorsey Press, 1976.

Young, Joseph, ed. *Federal Employees Almanac 1980*. Federal Employees News Digest, Inc., 1980.

Articles

Advertising Age. "Defense Ads to Top $144 Million." December 15, 1980.

Anderson, Jack. "Odyssey of A Diode: 32 Cents to $114." Syndicated column published in the *Washington Post*, February 17, 1981.

Anderson, Jack. "Watchdog Unit Gets Kicked in the Teeth." Syndicated column published in the *Washington Post*, September 25, 1980.

Bonafede, Dom. "Uncle Sam: The Flimflam Man?" *Washington Journalism Review*, April-May 1978.

Bredemeier, Kenneth. "A Powerless Group Influences the Shape of the City." *Washington Post*, July 6, 1980.

Bryant, Tim. "The FTC: A Fount of Business Data." Freedom of Information Center Report 409, University of Missouri School of Journalism, September 1979.

Clines, Francis. "State Department Briefing: Wagnerian and Risky." *New York Times*, February 12, 1981.

Congressional Quarterly Weekly Report. "Executive Branch Lobbying." August 2, 1980.

Farnsworth, Clyde. "Reagan Signs Order to Curb Regulations." *New York Times*, February 18, 1981.

Gamarekian, Barbara. "Washington Business: Keeping Track of the Bureaucrats." *New York Times*, January 4, 1981.

Gervasi, Tom. "The Doomsday Beat." *Columbia Journalism Review*, May-June 1979.

Gup, Ted, and Neumann, Jonathan. "Government Out of Control: Contracts." *Washington Post*, June 22-26, 1980.

Herbers, John. "$100 Billion Is Found Approved But Unused in Public Works Plans." *New York Times*, June 30, 1980.

Hilts, Phillip. "Agencies Rush Rules to Beat Inaugural Gun." *Washington Post*, January 18, 1981.

Jackson, Brooks. "Rub-a-Dub-Dub: Soon You Can Build a Bath Without Tub." *Wall Street Journal*, December 23, 1980.

Kalin, Steve. "Access to NRC Records." Freedom of Information Center Report 406, University of Missouri School of Journalism, July 1979.

Kast, Sheilah. "Auto Rules Piling Up—Car Regulation Study May Become Hit List." *Washington Star*, January 18, 1981.

Knight, Jerry. "SEC Probes Hunt Brothers' Bank Dealings." *Washington Post*, March 5, 1981.

Kurtz, Howie. "Job Switch Raises Conflict Questions for Ex-FAA Official." *Washington Star*, December 28, 1980.

Kurtz, Howie. "Reagan Hit on Firings of Inspectors General." *Washington Star*, January 22, 1981.

Love, Thomas. "Nominee for Transportation Post Puts Net Worth At $2.77 Million." *Washington Star*, January 8, 1981.

Love, Thomas. "Supplier Sold Untested Parts to Pentagon." *Washington Star*, December 11, 1980.

McCombs, Phil. "Rise and Fall of a Bureaucrat." *Washington Post*, November 9, 1980.

Miller, Annetta. "A Guide to the FDA." Freedom of Information Center Report 407, University of Missouri School of Journalism, July 1979.

Morris, Roger. "Carter's Cabinet: The Who's Who Treatment." *Columbia Journalism Review*, March-April 1977.

Morris, Roger. "Reporting for Duty: The Pentagon and the Press." *Columbia Journalism Review*, July-August 1980.

Perry, James. "Blue-Blood Choices Give Reagan Cabinet Establishment Tint." *Wall Street Journal*, December 24, 1980.

Randolph, Deborah. "Consultant Industry Thriving in Capital, But Reagan's Arrival Makes Some Nervous." *Wall Street Journal*, December 31, 1980.

Reed, Leonard. "The Budget Game and How to Win It." *Washington Monthly*, January 1979.

Reed, Leonard. "The Velvet Cage: The Life of a GS-15." *Washington Monthly*, September 1979.

Rich, Spencer. "Last-Minute Job Grants Probed." *Washington Post*, March 4, 1981.

Risser, James. Sixty-eight articles about corruption in the grain export trade. *Des Moines Register*, beginning May 4, 1975.

Rowen, Hobart. "America's Most Powerful Private Club." *Harper's*, September 1960.

Sawyer, Kathy. "Uncle Sam's New Look: A Workforce in Transition From Clerks to Technocrats." *Washington Post*, August 4, 1980.

Shanahan, Eileen. "Tips From a Former Flack." *Washington Journalism Review*, June-July 1979.

Shaplen, Robert. "Profiles—David Newsom." *The New Yorker*, June 2, June 9 and June 16, 1980.

Sinclair, Ward. "NIH Official Delivers a Waist-High Pitch on Budget." *Washington Post*, October 17, 1980.

Sylvester, Kathleen. "FCC Adopts Regulations Governing Its Communications." *Washington Star*, June 12, 1980.

Von Hoffman, Nicholas. "Hodding Carter Tells (Almost) All." *Columbia Journalism Review*, November-December 1980.

Von Hoffman, Nicholas. "How Washington Works: What Every President Should Know." *Playboy*, November 1980.

Wehr, Elizabeth. "Cutting Fraud, Waste, Abuse Still High Reagan Priority But Not Balanced Budget Key." *Congressional Quarterly Weekly Report*, February 21, 1981.

Weinberg, Steve. "Five Easy Guides Through the Bureaucracy." *The Quill,* February 1980.

Wilson, Paul. "The FCC: A Research Tool." Freedom of Information Center Report 410, University of Missouri School of Journalism, September 1979.

Woodward, Steve. "Public Files of the SEC." Freedom of Information Center Report 408, University of Missouri School of Journalism, August 1979.

Chapter V

Books

Baum, Lawrence. *The Supreme Court.* Congressional Quarterly Press, 1981.

Denniston, Lyle. *The Reporter and the Law.* Hastings House, 1980.

Devol, Kenneth. *Mass Media and the Supreme Court.* Hastings House, 1976.

Douglas, William. *The Court Years, 1939-1975.* Random House, 1980.

Grey, David. *The Supreme Court and the News Media.* Northwestern University Press, 1968.

Rohde, David, and Spaeth, Harold. *Supreme Court Decision Making.* W.H. Freeman, 1976.

Wilkinson, J. Harvie III. *Serving Justice: A Supreme Court Clerk's View.* Charterhouse, 1974.

Witt, Elder, ed. *Guide to the United States Supreme Court.* Congressional Quarterly Inc., 1979.

Woodward, Bob, and Armstrong, Scott. *The Brethren.* Simon and Schuster, 1979.

Articles

Barbash, Fred. "Problems With Patents: Agency, Inventors Fight Court Battles." *Washington Post,* January 5, 1981.

Denniston, Lyle. "Blackmun Role in Pay Ruling Creates Puzzle." *Washington Star,* December 17, 1980.

Denniston, Lyle. "Burger Ends Coolness to the Press." *Washington Star,* February 8, 1981.

Denniston, Lyle. "HHS Secretary, Justice Clash Over Hospitals." *Washington Star,* December 19, 1980.

Des Moines Register. "Cloud Over High Court." Editorial, September 14, 1980.

Love, Thomas. "Shipper Fighting Puerto Rico." *Washington Star,*
    June 16, 1980.
Pear, Robert. "More Court Papers May Be Kept Secret." *New
    York Times,* June 20, 1980.
Poses, Jonathan. "The Court of Military Appeals Garners Pen-
    tagon's Wrath." *Enlisted Times,* May 1980.

Chapter VI.

Books

Alexander, Herbert. *Financing Politics.* Congressional Quarterly
    Press, 1980.
Berry, Jeffrey. *Lobbying for the People.* Princeton University Press,
    1977.
Congressional Quarterly Inc. *The Washington Lobby,* 1979.
Deakin, James. *The Lobbyists.* Public Affairs Press, 1966.
Goulden, Joseph. *The Superlawyers.* Dell, 1972.
Green, Mark. *The Other Government: The Unseen Power of
    Washington Lawyers.* Grossman, 1975.
Lipsen, Charles, with Lesher, Stephan. *Vested Interest.* Doubleday,
    1977.
Malbin, Michael, ed. *Parties, Interest Groups and Campaign
    Finance Laws.* American Enterprise Institute for Public Policy
    Research, 1980.
Ornstein, Norman, and Elder, Shirley. *Interest Groups, Lobbying
    and Policymaking.* Congressional Quarterly Press, 1978.

Articles

Barlas, Stephen. "Congressional Ratings: Let the Voters Beware!"
    Independent News Alliance, July 1, 1980.
Broadcasting. "The Washington Lawyer: Power Behind the Powers
    That Be," June 16, 1980.
Business Week. "The Unlikely Alliance Blocking Lobby Reform,"
    July 14, 1980.
Cloherty, Jack. "Seven Flacks for Seven Sisters." *Washington Jour-
    nalism Review,* January-February 1978.
Denniston, Lyle: "U.S. Has Had Fifty-Four Cases Like Billy's."
    Washington Star, July 28, 1980.
Diuguid, Lewis. "U.S. Probing Firm With Ties to Reagan."
    Washington Post, September 8, 1980.

Farnsworth, Clyde. "Washington: The People Who Work for the Japanese." *New York Times*, June 29, 1980.

Gordon, Michael. "The Image Makers in Washington—PR Firms Have Found a Natural Home." *National Journal*, May 31, 1980.

Halonen, Doug, Krumm, Jo Ellen, Ludvik, James, Moore, Ann and Seery, Tom. "What Inside Washington Reads." *Washingtonian*, January 1981.

Hunt, Albert. "Such Good Friends: Policy and Society in the Capital." *Wall Street Journal*, December 11, 1980.

Keller, Bill. "Castoff Congressmen Find More Money and Less Misery Lobbying Former Colleagues." *Congressional Quarterly Weekly Report*, December 27, 1980.

Keller, Bill, and Felton, John. "Ex-Members and Officials Find Lucrative Employment Representing Foreign Clients." *Congressional Quarterly Weekly Report*, August 9, 1980.

Kurtz, Howie. "The Califano Syndrome: An Ethics Issue." *Washington Star*, June 23-24, 1980.

Lee, Richard. "Society Wars." *Washingtonian*, December 1979.

Lewis, Pat. "When He Talks, Even E.F. Hutton Listens." *Washington Star*, December 3, 1980.

Lowndes, Jay. "Using IRS Form 990." *IRE Journal*, Winter 1980.

Nahin, Paul. "For Your Eyes Only." *Omni*, December 1980.

Nessen, Ron. "The Washington You Can't See on Television." *TV Guide*, September 20, 1980.

Pine, Art. "Quoth the Maven Now and Evermore." *Washington Post*, December 7, 1980.

Reilly, Ann. "Washington Information Boom." *Dun's Review*, March 1979.

Romano, Lois. "The Green Book Listings: Money Isn't Everything." *Washington Star*, March 3, 1981.

Rosselini, Lynn. "Capital Does as Reagans Do, Since Power Is Always In." *New York Times*, February 12, 1981.

Sachar, Emily. "Billion-Dollar Trade Associations: Area's Third Largest Employer. *Washington Post*, August 4, 1980.

Smardz, Zofia. "Memory Jogged by Conversation at Garden Party." *Washington Star*, July 26, 1980.

Yoffe, Emily. "The Domains of Eminence: Brookings and AEI." *Washington Journalism Review*, November 1980.

Chapter VII.

Books

Blumenthal, Sidney. *The Permanent Campaign: Inside the World of Elite Political Operatives.* Beacon Press, 1980.

Broder, David. *The Party's Over.* Harper & Row, 1972.

Crouse, Timothy. *The Boys on the Bus.* Ballantine Books, 1973.

Fairlie, Henry. *The Parties.* St. Martin's, 1978.

Fishel, Jeff, ed. *Parties and Elections in an Anti-Party Age.* Indiana University Press, 1978.

Goldwin, Robert, ed. *Political Parties in the Eighties.* American Enterprise Institute for Public Policy Research, 1980.

Harwood, Richard, ed. *The Pursuit of the Presidency Washington Post*/Berkeley, 1980.

McGinniss, Joe. *The Selling of the President 1968.* Trident, 1969.

Witcover, Jules. *Marathon: The Pursuit of the Presidency 1972-1976. Viking, 1977.*

Articles

Agranoff, Robert. "Campaign Management: Benefits of the Professional Approach." *Campaigns & Elections,* Spring 1980.

Broder, David. "A Victory Women Can Cheer." *Washington Post,* March 11, 1981.

Broder, David. "Reapportionment Fight: Republicans Ready Their Computers." *Washington Post,* March 10, 1981.

Clymer, Adam. "Republicans to Spend $1 Million on Efforts for Fair Redistricting." *New York Times,* March 1, 1981.

Frankel, Glenn, and Baker, Donald. "Robb, Coleman Ready Virginia Campaigns." *Washington Post,* March 15, 1981.

Germond, Jack, and Witcover, Jules. "Changing Signals." *Washington Star,* March 15, 1981.

Landauer, Jerry. "Congressmen Offer Access to Raise Cash." *Wall Street Journal,* August 6, 1980.

Logan, Gary. "A Guide to Media Consultants and Press Secretaries." *Washington Journalism Review,* September 1980.

Lyons, Richard. "Two Southerners Vying to Get Caucus Post." *Washington Post,* September 25, 1980.

Peterson, Bill. "GOP Mapping Multimillion-Dollar Fund Drives for Senate and House." *Washington Post,* March 5, 1981.

Roberts, Steven. "Congress Chiefs Predict Big Changes in Tax
    Plan." *New York Times*, March 10, 1981.
Walsh, Edward. "Bill Brock: Architect of Republican Revival."
    Washington Post, November 20, 1980.
Witcover, Jules. "DNC Critics Given Chance to Audit Committee's
    Books for Previous Four Years." *Washington Star*, December
    10, 1980.

Miscellaneous

Books

Babb, Laura, ed. *Washington Post Guide to Washington*. McGraw-
    Hill, 1978.
King, Anthony, ed. *The New American Political System*. American
    Enterprise Institute for Public Policy Research, 1978.
Kiplinger, Austin, with Kiplinger, Knight. *Washington Now*. Harper
    & Row, 1975.
Markel, Lester. *What You Don't Know Can Hurt You*.
    Quadrangle/New York Times, 1973.
Morehead, Joe. *Introduction to United States Public Documents*.
    Libraries Unlimited, 1978.
Murphy, Harry. *Where's What: Sources of Information for Federal
    Investigators*. Warner Books, 1976.
Peters, Charles. *How Washington Really Works*. Addison-Wesley,
    1980.
Peters, Charles, and Fallows, James, ed. *Inside the System*.
    Praeger, 1976.

Articles

Matusow, Barbara. "Researching Washington by Telephone." *The
    Masthead*, Summer 1980.

"To Get The Most Attention, You Have To Be Stacked The Right Way."

Index